FRIE

NDS

Corwin Peck
2014

FRIENDS

Sean Thomas Blott

Alec Regan
Michael Senise
Brad Troemel
Scott Dickson
Ken Kagami
Alex Savage
Kristi O'Meara
Cody James Frei
Tim S
Joshua Citarella
J Goudreault
Sean Joseph Patrick Carney
Lauren Christiansen
Casey Colgan
Paul Smith
Mitchell Hugh Kirkwood
Michelle Grabner
Lea Griggs
Joshua T Howell
John Riepenhoff
Dylan Mortimer
Ryder Ripps
Andrew William Erdrich
Elise Hanson
Josh Reames
Nick Missel
Lauren Taylor
Madeline Gallucci
Braden Baer
Joshua Ramirez
Tyson Reeder
Laura Volkert
Willy Carpenter
Oliver Sydello
Sofia Leiby
Milton Frazier Stevenson V
Reece Ousey
Rose Tarman
Justin Schulte
Bradly Doyle Fischer
Matt Jacobs
Tyler Roberts
Alicia Lantzy
Jordan Johnson
Molly Kaderka
Andrew Lyles
Yeah Ball
Ashley Janke
Kelly Mattimoe
Molly Rhinestones
Robert Chase Heishman

Shane Walsh
Morgan Manduley
Jordan Brethauer
Neil Thrun
Huey Crowley
Valentina Zamfirescu
Jan Dolo
Jeff Morrison
Miki Baird
Richard Galling
Stephanie Leedy
Brian Nigus
Robert J. Baumann
Tito Dixon
Ahram Park
Carly Huibregtse
Kevin Wells
Tyler Dawson
Karl Saffran
L Cool Brad J
Jon Rafman
Jenna Knapp
Sovannra Yos
Claire Ashley
Elizabeth Allen-Cannon
Spencer Sweeney
Joshua Abelow
Colby Cusick
Jake Rathkamp
Amy Trompeter
Jillian Kay
Alexandra Gorczynski
Julio César Cordova
Dusty Colyer
Sean Weber
Marianne Laury
Petra Cortright
Brett W/ Schultz
Autumn Elizabeth Clark
Jakki Cafarelli
Katy McRoberts
Lydia Jarvis
Ben Miller
Xavier Ruffin
Jeremy Bena
David Hughes
Nate Pyper
Brittany Ellenz
Katie Batten
Nicholas Nagowski
Sarie Omen

Cara Corder
Jason Comotto
Erin Riggins
Angela Marie Ferch
Melissa Dorn Richards
Ian Sonsyadek
Amber A. Krueger
Erica Flannery
Gretchen Solinger
James Pederson
Priscilla Whitenight
Liza Pflughoft
Andrija Dolter
Tess Doyle
Abi Shaw
Steven J. Cromwell
Sara Bott
Brett Henzig
Sam Foster
Katie Kreger
Richard Grimm
Chris Biddy
Bryan Nathaniel Knotts
Marisa de la Peña
Heather Lamanno
Debra Brehmer
Krystal Kuhn
Peter Granados
KyLe Vvis
Katlyn Ross
Kelly Walker
Paul Cowan
CJ Schrat
Tom Owens
Calvin Whitehurst
Skully Skyrocket
Tony R
Bryan Jones
Dan Bellia
Cory Imig
Utrecht Milwaukee
Sean M. Starowitz
Deb Leal
Katie Grace Atkins
Beverly Ahern
Kz Purp
Andrew Michael Harting
Ila Medlin
Joseph Reeves
Kate Perryman
Chelsea Wynn

Robert Josaiah Bingaman	Nicole Mauser	Anthony Veale
Miles Fermin	Jacob Muselmann	Jim Woodfill
Utrecht Miad	Ann Leachman	Michael Kautzer
Molly Simmons Radke	Julioe Aniela Sikonski	Sakari Singh
Andrew Azad	Paul Druecke	Michael Manning
Michael Garrett	Sara Caron	Travess Smalley
Ian Tirone	Thomas A. Luna	Jesse Stone
Annie Raab	Sean Kelley	Dana McNeil
Chris Daharsh	Happy Collaborationists	Eric Frank
Michael Mahalchick	Generally Luke Hall	Riley Plemons
Kevin Bland	Anthony Antonellis	Malcolm Lee
Mark Moran	Brady Wells	Barr Jasonn
Neil Gasparka	Evan Davies	Jenny Roberts
Asheer Akram	Timothy Contie	Alice Huang
Rachel De Joode	Mary-Louise Schumacher	Ann Hirsch
Mike Ketchpaw	Max Crutcher	Guthrie Lonergan
Blair Schulman	Francis Rivera Jr.	Michael Adams
Cheryl Santos	Anna Vining	Rollin Leonard
Derek Frech	Thomas Hellstrom	Amanda Maria
Brett Ginsburg	Amanda Martinez	Rachel Bock
Michael Davidson	Amanda Browder	Katherine Pill
Brian Fisch	Parker Ito	Amanda Uhlers
Jacque TreeHorn	Mossy Dew	Ricky Allman
Peter Halley	Avery Peña	Zak Keir
Bruce Hartman	Molly Rhinestones	Derek Paul Boyle
Megan Colyer	Chris Simpson	Matthew Schoenauer
Eric Thomas Wolever	Anthony Baab	Barry Rogers
Amy J Kligman	Ashley Morgan	Justin Kernen
Jason Lazarus	Quinn Reeder	Brittany Biedenbender
Wendy White	Lance Ryan Heybrock	Ron Wickersham
Dean Roper	Kari Freitag	Adam Jensen
Sabina Ott	Craig Howard	Sarah Magaña
Andrew Norman Wilson	Mike Becker	Diane Heise
Jamilee Polson Lacy	Joshua Ferdinand	Natasha Robbins
Dennis Helsel	Dustin Downey	Shayna Ice Cream Cohn
Colin Joseph Burke	Carla Malone Steck	Tim Conley
T Oliver Sweet	Scott Reeder	Elisabeth Redmon Albeck
Dave Rhoads	Ross Redmon	Nicholas hense
John Kowalczyk	Zach Rensberger	Tyler Nikolas
Sara Krajewski	Galia Basail	Jennifer Chan
Jeremy Morehead	Peter Ibsen	Alexandria Fredrickson
Tome Robertes	Steven Gorman	Mike Bertrandt
Kris Belden-Adams	Elysia Borowy-Reeder	Brian VanSpakeren
Gillian Tobin	Timothy Bergstrom	Erik Liimatta
Austin Montee	Abdi Farah	Matt Watts
Conor Backman	Jena Lee	Jordan Elsberry
Sweaty Theodore Esala	Jonah Criswell	Paige Welch
Nick Matthews	Corwin Peck	Rachel Hoffman
David Ford	Hank Hafkemeyer	Amanda Lynn
Isaac Russell Brethauer	Sarah Gail Luther	Rachel Niffenegger-Tinder
Aaron Storck	Interstake BK	Garrett Mohr

Clayton Skidmore
Keith J Weller
Youming Chen
Elizabeth Jaeger
Davin Underwood
Leone Reeves
Eric Hollub
Thorne Brandt
Nicholas H.K. Falcone
Anna Toms
Mary Colleen
Sharmaine Perea
Emily Troxell
Katie Bell
Matt Hilfer
Katherina Dimenstein
Brian Henkel
Kevin Howdeshell
Hailey Loman
Juice Wick
Lauren Jones
Hanah Mor
Stephanie Richardson
Joe Lawlor
Chris Kiefer
Jake Wiens
Amy Compton
Mattheus Alexander Jebediah Leonhard
Mark Conner
Leila Hinkle
Donald W Pelton IV
Christina Dostaler Prestidge
Chloe Mann
Terry Campbell
Branwen Cromer
Tyra Forker
Yasmine Niazi
Evan Hill.
Emmanuel Amido
Ben McLaughlin
Sarah Hope Miller
Micah Lidberg
Charlotte Enders
Tabor Robak
Chelsea Short
Osciel Ramos
Sara Cramer
Brandy Lee Harter
Shawn Michael Eklund
Josh Brielmaier

Thom Webb
Kyle Schryver
Genia Narinskaya
Sampson James
Adam McCambridge
Malory Ward
Kevin Berg
Megan Sullivan
Daniel Goggin
Jarod Johnson
Rachel Valinsky
Brandon Rodenbeck
James Meyer
Carmen Moreno
MacKeag Resh
Mark Yatchak
May Tveit
Justin Blake Barnett
Michael Thompson
Anna Kamerer
Joe Taylor
Kyle Swanson
Scott Pipal
Julian Chams
Jarrod Gaffney
Shane Jezowski
Matthew Dehaemers
Joe Keesee
Tyler Fleshman
Tony Matelli
Aurora Kettering
Marcus Traber
Eric Andrew Breber
Bethany Martinez
Beck Traver
Alison Trent
Annie Woodfill
Jesse Stecklow
Clifford Owens
Holly Swangstu
Sarah Smith
Nicholas Wylie
Chad Machajewski
Travis Achilles Webb
Stewart Losee
Eddie Villanueva
Mark Mansingh
Emily Connell
Philip Gresham
Sara Rinehart
Christine Stormberg

Aramis Gutierrez
Katie Bear Adams
Elaine McMilian
Yosi Sergant
Joe Hamilton
Joe K Fuller
Tobias Madison
Justin Janowski
Emily Catherine
Andy Maugh
Ashley Anders
Young Sun Han
Rashid Johnson
Ra Sh Awn Griffin
Bill Brady
Penelop Umbrico
Brennan Ponder
Scott Hug
Davin Watne
Rachael Grandon
Colby Smith
Kevin McNally
Kristin Calabrese
Sara Jimenez
Alby Maccarone
Casey Colgan
Ben Holt
Jordan Janowski
Rachel Rolon
Nathan David Schultz
Lola Rose Thompson
Nathan Falcone
David Harrison
Elisa Harkins
Wyatt Lewis
Maria Elena Buszek
Amos Leager
Brett Reif
Sherry Leedy
Lyssandra Gallup
Bo Jack Laxton
Darker Knight
Byron Cohen
Kadar Brock
Jim Sajovic
Anne Austin Pearce
Sarynn Anderson
Jose Lerma
Hugh Merrill
Micah K Barta
Evan Gruzis

Nick Marx
Ryan Timothy Laferney
Crosby Kemper
Ben Anderson
Lillie Schenk
Kate Hackman
Matt Cygnet
Duncan MacKenzie
Michael Krueger
Jordan Fox
Michelle Kozubek
Jesse Kappell
Shinique Smith
Alika Cooper
Jonas Lund
Bill Haw
Cary Esser
Shana Moulton
Peregrine Honig
Caroline Sulek
Josh DiMaggio
Vincent Uribe
Brandon Forrest Frederick
Michael Staniak
Jarrett Mellenbruch
Rachel Marie
Austin Lee
Bri Chesler
Aron Gent
Robby Perry
Amanda Ross-Ho
Waseem Touma
Roger Shimomura
Wyatt Wood
Jackie Saccoccio
Traci Gray Ketter
Amanda Elise Bowles
Sarita Mahinay
Lee Piechocki
Stephanie Bloodgood
Grant W Miller
Austin Buckingham
Joe Bussell
Abed Said
Annabelle Arlie
David Brookins
Russel Hombs
Russell Shoemaker
Wu Tsang
Richard Holland
Misty Gamble

Whitney Leigh
Emily Shudy
Lorna Mills
Sarah Faye McPherson
Jeremy Bolen
Hal Wert
Json Myers
Garrett Fuselier
Peggy Noland
Sean Minor
Tex Jernigan
Vahid Sharifian
Dean Daderko
Nate Reiners
Timothy Bukowski
Genji Kobayashi
Mike Sinclair
Kelsey Smith
Maria Kamutzki
Mat Engelhardt
Caranne Camarena
Ayla Rexroth
Corinna Kirsch
Dan 'Danny' Orendorff
Martijn Hendriks
Mike Zippel
Aaron Graham
Eg Schempf
Katy Putlitz
Kelly Cegielski
Michael Bond
Micah Andrew Moore
Deanna Diekman
Andrew Lyles
Cara Megan lewis
Ben Harle
Kate Clements
Rob Pruitt
Forrest Nash
Anthony Nissen
Anthony Hurlburt
Kris Rowinski
Caitlin Halstead
Chet Allen
Judith G. Levy
Larry Thomas
Tory Fiolliard
King S-Blaze Tell Em
Kate Smithson
Christopher Lineberry
Brad Deal

Kathy Cho
Jon Miller
Kaylee Fitzgibbons
Eddie Williams
John Michael Boling
Jules de Balincourt
Jacob Moore
Tim Morales
John Obrien
Erika Lynne Hanson
Emily Kay Henson
Jake Ludemann
Joey Embers
Electro Mayo
Zhang Zin Yue
Luke Shelton
Jayne Elyzabeth Montgomery
Haley Wilson
Will Anderson
Leedy-Voulkos Art Center
Jonas Wood
Keyan Alemifar
Jessica Marak
Chris Frye
Kendra Werst
Aaron Esala
Isaac AhLoe
Archie Gobber
Katie Davenport
Steve Lewis
Andy Montee
Kyle Christopher Beck
Dilan Effinger
Charlie Smith
Allayne Thornton
Joseph F. Wilson II
Jacob Thatface Schildtknecht
Lottie Barker
Jessica Brackett
Paul Tyler
Block Artspace
Travis Pratt
Kyle Samuelson
Linda Buchlinger
Henry Klimowicz
Chandler Ervin Charles Quinn
Andrew Rafacz
Tyler Owens
Raechell Smith
Christopher Bell
Mike Erickson

Teal Wilson
Brandon Barr
Michael Rooks
Susan White
Stephanie Sterling
Max Newman
Lydia Boehr DeMonte
McKenzie Marston
Taj Bourgeois
Kory Tyler
Robert Brandon Eastham
Ron Ewert
Maegen Stracy
Alexander Lee Porter
Patrick Stout
Carrie Riehl
Sheri Vining
Shabahang Tayyari
Justin Fakemiddlename Hansen
Shae Bishop
Jen Watson
Benjamin Lyman
Karen McCoy
KC Utrecht
Misako Rosen
Marcie Miller Gross
Kent Michael Smith
Brandon Waltman
Bill Thelen
Dan Motanye
Skye Livingston
Yesi Castillo
Mark Voelz
Zac James Heimdale
Stacy Switzer
Bob Jones
Nick Kanter
Christopher M Wilson
Sara Geach
Rhiannon Birdsall
Alex Prudic-dennis
Cordy Mickowski
Chuck Lees
Thomas Linder
Jenny Wustmann
Matt Waters
Ian Smith
Brittany Krumbeck
Vicky Bates
Chris Salani

Matt Walby
Michael Schonhoff
Steve Brisendine
Chelsea Lehmann
Erik Dahl
Skyler Bierberly
Peter Panos
Dave Dumay
Samantha Kroll
Diane Scott
Katie Kobs
Jason D. Harris
Marcus Cain
Keith Simpson
Michael Bell-Smith
Erwin Wurm
Kelly John Clark
Colin Matthes
Sixty-Second Dimension
Matt Wycoff
Eric Kremin
Exis Arts Mary Braun
Marc Fischer
Michael Thibault
Shaman R Shaman
Shawn Robinson
Printosaurus Roar
Theo Dore Bunch
J.t. Warren
Kris Adams
Fox Theis
Nicole Retmman Soliz
Jolene Gabriel
Damien Hirst
Blake Sidebottom
Alex Phillips
Eric Fischle
Dan Arps
Nicholas Naughton
S'mores Cart
David Kobzantsev
Jay Canty
Daniel Avazpour
Stephen Proski
Spencer Peterson
Adam Kuhnen
Brenna Murphy
Kelton Labs
Will Anderson
Georgia Hamhockin-turkey Lef-teaspoon Moon
Julie Malen

Tim Lenhart
Sean D'Andrade
New Capital
Dringus Dangle
Balm Art
Cameron Cornwell
Ella Dwyer
Nevada WOlf
Ciara Embach Ruffino
Mel Chen
Brand Troemel
Jenny Strand
Parker Chee To
Freddie Wyss
Dinos Chapman
Painter Vs Painting
Peter Ibsen
Anton KernGallery
Tony Oppenheimer
Tessa Reuber

Andrew Durbin

Josef Kaplan
CA Conrad
Lauren Christiansen
Ian Hatcher
Lønely Christopher
Zachary German
Stephen Boyer
Brad Troemel
James La Marre
Ed Halter
Ariana Reines
Kate Durbin
Jacolby Satterwhite
Kevin Killian
Same Text
Ben Fama
Adam Fitzgerald
Juliana Huxtable
Andrew Kenower
Sophia Le Fraga
Jamie Sterns
Brandon Brown
Audrey Zee Whitesides
Ryan Doyle May
Artie Vierkant
Brad Wilson
Jacob Brown
Judah Steadicam Rubin
Thom Donovan
Jacob Steinberg
Dana Ward
Vanessa Plaza
Mauzy Virgina
David Knowles
Diana Sue Hamilton
Joshua Citarella
Bianca Stone
Sampson Starkweather
Mark Johnson
Stuart Comer
Sasha Fletcher
Hilton Als
Leopoldine Core
John Galvin
Jenny Zhang
Jennifer Tamayo
David Davis
Alexander Provan
Jan St Eustache
Joyelle McSweeney
Anna Anna Vitale

Ben Pease
Trisha Low
Omar Kholeif
Rachel Kushner
Bunny Rogers
Evan Kennedy
Charity Coleman
Avis Elizabeth
David Blumenshine
Nicole Reber
Marcus McDonald
Erin Morrill
Katie Degentesh
Trace Peterson
Thomas Beard
Ricardo Domeneck
Brendan Lorber
Katy Bohinc
Peter J. Russo
Alaina Stamatis
Julian Yuri Rodriguez
Dodie Bellamy
Tan A. Lin
Keith J. Varadi
Eric Conroe
Amy King
Lawrence Schwartzwald Tran
Angelo Nikolopoulos
Matvei Yankelevich
Shelby Jackson
Paige Taggart
Shiv Kotecha
Alina Gregorian
Sam Frank
Giampaolo Bianconi
Eric Linkser
Dorothy Howard
Chris Alexander
Brik Olson
Sue Landers
Kristen Gallagher
Simone Kearney
Ted Dodson
Benjamin Barron
Ian Aleksander Adams
Caroline Gormley
Ann Hirsch
Evander Batson
Cammisa Buerhaus
Gabe Hoot

Rachel Burns
Jocelyn Spaar
Eileen Myles
Thor Shannon
Ryan McGinnis
Emily Pettit
Eric Nelson
Holly Melgard
Ben Rosenberg
Theodore Kerr
Rachel B. Glaser
Jac Alx Wad
Joseph Massey
Joey Yearous-Algozin
Travis Meyer
Paul Mpayi Sepuya
Emily Hunt
Tom Healy
Stephen Motika
Mark Leidner
Colin Self
Michael Valinsky
Jonathan Liebembuk
Editrice de Nineteenthirteen
Genji Amino
Maria Damon
Michael Barron
Olivier Green
Joe Luna
Ian Dreiblatt
Dan Magers
Ed Fornieles
Matt Nelson
Julian Smith-Newman
Rob Halpern
Chris Hosea
Guy Pettit
Mickey Mahar
Luke Gilford
Wendy Lotterman
Goro II
Photios Giovanis
Joon Lee
Mark Bibbins
Ross Leonardy
Eric Schwartau
Stacey Tran
Ara Shirinyan
Donnie Jochum
Marcel Alcalá
Walter Davis

Nathan Lee
Joseph Mosconi
David Fishkind
Isabella Glaudini
Allen Edwin Butt
Brian Droitcour
Carolyn Lazard
John Brnlv Rogers
Chris Nealon
Dorrito Malandrino
Drew Krewer
Douglas A. Martin
Matt Wolf
Jesse N Ov A
Jos Charles
Grayson Wolf
Mx Bean
Jon Rutzmoser
Lucy Ives
Tedd Fluffqvist Trees
Jennifer Nelson
Bjarne Melgaard
Sam McKinniss
Cassandra Gillif
Megan Ewing
Stephen Cook
Brandon Downing
Sophia Dahlin
Jack Schneider
Jamee Ernst
Jacob Severn
Andrew Norman Wilson
Jeff Grunthaner
Jw McCormack
Bradford Morrow
Lucas Allan Bumgart
Libby Riefler
Ari Spool
Ira Silverberg
James Sherry
Matthew Timmons
Max Steele
Taj Bourgeois
Ally Davis
Ben Tripp
Brian Stefans
Michael Thomas Vassallo
JiaJia Fei
Harold Abramowitz
Jamie Townsend
Drrty Pharms

Russ Aplacebothwonder-
fulandstrange Marshalek
Michael Nicoloff
Jason Zuzga
Nicholas Andre Sung
Erica Kaufman
Negative Copy
Lara Glenum
Alex Dimitrov
Ryder Ripps
Miley Stafford
Ken K. Walker
Logan Jackson
Robert Whitehead
Daniel Tiffany
Christian Letourneau
Broq Robinson
Ann Lauterbach
Francine Prose
Roger Van Voorhees
Zachary de la Fox
Victoria Vreeland
Amy Silbergeld
Lysette Elizabeth Simmons
Catie Scott
Dana Howard
Heather Durbin
Andrew Dieck
Danielle Sinay
Noah Chasin
Sarah Sarai
Jake Stortini
Daniella Rose King
Michael Anzuoni
Parker Ito
NP Jaeger
Kasey Mohammad
Kitty Mcguire
Lauren Cornell
Stephanie Boluk
Carl Williamson
Nellie Killian
Kathy Harris
Camille Bertrand
Yasmine Lucas
Andrew Maxwell
Wyatt Niehaus
Maggie Wells
Heiko Julien
Josh Aleksanyan
Timothy Donnelly

Geoff Wallace
Kyle Bella
Lisa Marie Basile
Divya Victor
Greg Curtis
Geneviève Belleveau
Jane Stephens Rosenthal
Deric Carner
Melissa Broder
Sammi Bryan
Erika Staiti
Rachael Williams
Gil Lawson
Joshua Lyon
Tommy Pico
Jillian Mayermayermayer
Doreothea Lasky
Andrew Shuta
Gio Black Peter
Rod Smith
Anselm Berrigan
Christie Ann Reynolds
Nicholas Von Kleist
Hitomi Yoshio
Sebastian Cheron
Keith Gray
Monica McClure
Jamie Bayard
Theodore Hanna
Tony Bordonaro
Matias Viegener
Samuel Delany
Michael J Seidlinger
Jerome Rothenberg
Julian Talamantez Brolaski
Everett Freeman Hamilton
Kerry Barron
Ana Cecilia Alvarez
Zak Kitnick
Lucian Wintrich
Amy Lawless
Travis Holloway
Eliott Glass
Kylan Rice
Steven Karl
Edwin Ramoran
Abigail Durbin
Alana Siegel
Liz Clark Wessel
Laurie Weeks
Alan Felsenthal

Fred P Hochberf
Charles Bernstein
Jacob Perkins
Krystal Languell
Chris Martin
Patrick Gaughan
Sara Larsen
Donald Dunbar
Alexandra Whitehill Smith
Uche Nduka
Michael Blum
Nick Faust
Jack Frost
Brooklyn Kat
Moira Donegan
Arthur Seefahrt
Lancelot Runge
Brenda Iijima
O'clock Press
Michelle Tea
Torito Toro
Michael David Quattlebaum Jr
Alli Warren
Juan M Amaya
Robert Richburg
Nada Gordon
Gracie Leavitt
James Yeh
Shana Celi
Lincoln Michel
Jessica Lebovits
Hugo Martinez
Emmalae Russo
Marisa Olson
Teresa Carmody
Alan Gilbert
Jemma Gallagher
Ben Estes
Ignis Feuerbrand
Jeremy Bailey
Natalie Eilbert
Mamie Morgan
P. Scott Cunningham
Benjamin Eldon Stevens
Caroline Alexander
Emily Skillings
Laura Brown
Frances Richard
Lawrence Giffin
Don Share
Dave Pekerow

Mary E. Richard
Leore Smurphy
Laura Woltag
Hari Hains
Greg Newton
Myer Mendelson
Clara Lipfert
Hedi El Kholti
Carleen Tibbetts
Morgan Eriksson
Mikey D Lane
Commune Editions
Mike Lala
Aaron Beasley
Patrick Belaga
Ruth Lichtman
Mark Fletcher
Kiely Sweatt
Ryan Revell
Aurora Linnea
David Sakover
John Giorno
Matthew Emmanuel Fee
Drew Scott Swenhaugen
Lucy Schmid
Cathey Anderson
Robert Gluck
Daniel Jumbotron Files
Anna Moschovakis
Becca Klaver
Steve Dickison
Shanice Anne Castle-Maudette
Ashlyn Silkiner
Emily Brandt
Josh Hodge
Zoë Elizabeth Noyes
Kim Calder
Mary Jean Murphy
Edmund Berrigan
Frank Sherlock
Paul Wagenblast
Glenn Barret Gallagher
Adam Humphreys
Mahbod Moghadam
Cynthia Sailers
Marshall Walker Lee
Spencer Madsen
Bex Blakely
Dan Callahan
Raphael Faerystar
Emily Ussery

Macy Rodman
Jamar Williams
Sandrinista Isabel
Elias Bender Roønnenfelt
Maria Celis
Joshua Furst
Cosmic Jardin
Joseph A. W. Quintela
Evanie Fraust
Ryan Murphy
Richard Siken
Sam Green
Titi Phan
Sara Kornhauser
Diana Tourjee
Christine Neacole
Kanownik
Claire E. Peters
Sam Roberts
Evan Gelion
David James Miller
Lizzie Baur
Eric Brown
Elaine Kahn
Kevin Christophers
Andrew Gorin
Carina Finn
Eric Niehaus
Heather Christle
Felix Amber
Karen Lepri
Geoffrey Billetter
David Gorin
Isaiah Swanson
Knusper Flakes
Ben Mirov
Miles Joris-Peyrafitte
Margaret Jennings
Jedediah Berry
Lucas de Lima
Alex Key
David Wolach
Lauren Koch
Beach Sloth
Tori Cole
Johannes Göransson
Luma Stiftung
Paul Foster Johnson
Sharon Monroe
Kelly Stuart
Lucas Sams

Amanda Montei
Kristine Kruta
Aaron Green
Kit Schluter
Ana Božicević
Danielle Pafunda
Paul W. Bennett IV
Brian Joseph
Corina Copp
Daniel Schwartž
Jessica Jernigan
Michelle Betters
Karen Wiser
Sara Jane Stoner
Jesse White
Mira Gonzalez
Iris Cushing
Michael Joseph Ernst
Kae Thee Smith
Amaranth Borsuk
Abby Marie Pfeiffer
Chesley Polk
Paul Stephens
Rob Fitterman
Ben Roylance
Macgregor Card
Jameson Fitzpatrick
Sarah Gerard
Emily Toder
Abraham Adams
Tom Comitta
Lanny Jordan Jackson
Cecilia K Corigan
David Everitt Howe
Gabe Kruis
Kevin Cassem
Matt Longabucco
Jeff Nagy
Chris Kraus
Felix Bernstein
Danny Snelson
Eric Amling
Jacqueline Waters
Sean Zhuraw
Carolyn Bush
Dolan Morgan
Juice Boxshi
Janey Smith
Trent Barnes
Paul Legault
Jay Deshpande

Asher Lewis
Al Filreis
Michael Walek
Interstate BK
Farnoosh Fathi
Shawn Wen
Kevin Mcgarrt
Unnameable Boox
Victoria Cho
Chris Richards
Forsyth Harmon
Janice Lee
Erin O'Brian
Michelle Taransky
Colby Chamberlain
Rafa Garcia Febles
Ricardo Maldonado
Zachary Davis
Alex Halpern Levy
Stephanie Berger
Ralph Schaefer
Alex Bacon
Marina Weiss
Joshua Edward
Mike Fu
David Weisberg
Rachel Silveri
Lily Ladewig
Lynn Xu
Joss Lake
Clairborne McDonald
Leah Schrager
Mary Austin Speaker
George Bennett
Hoa Nguyen
Michael D Snediker
Brian Hewes
Dane Terry
Tristan Hoffmann
Shannon Scott
Lauren Hunter
Brooks Sterritt
Spencer Longo
Julia Cohen
Ross Wolfe
Laura Jean Moore
Stephen Tullu Dierks
Dawn Lundy Martin
Jacob Perkins
Lisa Ciccarello
Angela Washko

Patrick Allan
Samantha Zighelboim
Tim Jones-Yelvington
Stefan Sirucek
Jeremy Bauer
Marina Blitshteyn
Claire Donato
Paul Vogel
Alex Greenberg
Sean Monahan
Roberto Montes
Johnny Sagan
Adam McLachlan
josh mosh
Megan Boyle
Matthew Broggini
Taylor Jacob Pate
Stephen Burt
Kate Litterer
Brooke Ellsworth
Patrick Conway
Molly Schaeffer
Taylor Darwin
Mark J Estrada
Danniel Schoonebeek
Lizzy Crawford
Dustin Luke Nelson
Matthew Sherling
Cameron Ogg
Zachary Pace
Michelle Sinsky
Jordan Scott
Alexander Nelson Wright
D Period Gilson
Alex Hampshire
Nick Sturm
Jessica Loudis
Vanessa Haroutunian
Shelly Rosenberg
Anne Cecelia Holmes
Sam Roeck
Amanda Martinez
Kendra Grant Malone
Casey Hannan
Rachel Rabbit White
Mike Young
Nick Scholl
Rachel Valinsky
Ben Richmond
Jason Yost
Logan Fry

Kate Robinson	Ryan McNamara	Andrew Sheaf
Elias Van Son	Dan Machlin	Ash Hall
De Se	Temnete Mesgun Sebhatu	Aubrie Marrin
Laura Henriksen	Natalie Lyalin	Marjon Carlos
John Tuite	Joseph Mains	Ross Satterfield
Neon Glittery	Ben Lerner	Mónica De La Torre
Alex Ross	Margaret Sands	Brandon Whitmore
Leon Strictlybusiness	Stephen Green	Timmothy Rushton
Walker	Martin Rock	Jared Wells
Taran Allen	Stephanie Ann Whited	Anthony Madrid
Blake Butler	Amanda Deutsch	Sheet Tooth
Julian Chams	Thomas Devaney	Veronique Whittaker
Ethan Osten	Laura Minor	Carrie Frey
Yvette Siegert	Sophie Cabot Black	Kitty Joe Sainte-Marie
Kate McCluskey	Gina Myers	Gabriel Helio Sanchez
Jon Ruseski	Jack Nachmanovitch	Miguel Murphy
Dan Hoy	Marina Galperina	Katy Henriksen
Eliza Dunaway	Jeffery Berg	Katy Lederer
Valentina VK	Mahwish Tazeem	Patrick Ferroni
Celeste Cass	Cate Marvin	Kim Vodicka
Efthalia Papacosta	Glen Fogel	Cameron Blaylock
Maryrose Larkin	Carlos Motta	Sofia de Guzman
Will Janowitz	Duke Riley	Kathleen Miller
Hari Nef	Mårten Wessel	Will Rahilly
Manon Manavit	Christopher DeWeese	Joaquin Gregorio
Mark Lamoureux	Kazim Ali	Linda Chen
Chadwick Redden	Francesca Capone	Noelle Willecke
Justin Marks	Amanda Ackerman	Ken Babstock
Randy Leo	Nina Johnson-Milewski	Lazy Daze
Joe Pan	Stephen Elliott	Ciege Cagalawan
Brian Spears	Caroline McTeer	Sylvia Mae Gorelick
Matilde Daviu	Braden Joyce-Schleimer	Blake C. Scott
Billy Merrell	Jayme Karales	Debrah Morkun
Snow Leopard Trek	Eric Baus	Tamira Raziel Cahana
Carlos Pintado	Fernando Garcia	Rauan Klassnik
Christopher Salerno	Yesenia Garcia	Donte Sagan Jung
Mitch Taylor	Phillipe Via	Steamtrain
Jared White	Chris Tonelli	Nicholas van Eck
Leigh Stein	Jamie Be	Carter Edwards
Laura Goldstein	Barbe Brown Morris	Thibault Lac
Robert Grand	Shanna Compton	Jackie Clark
Ali Power	Sarah Pelch	Lesser Gonzalez
Clay Banes	Ginosko Literary Journal	Daniel Poppick
Oliver Herbert	Ashley Warlick	Jane Gregory
Corrine Fitzpatrick	Joel W Henderson	Elizabeth Cordingley
Johann Kolstrup	Suzanne Stein	Maya Weeks
Christopher Stoddard	Stuart Krimko	Bea De la Cruz
Ron Silliman	Prabarna Ganguly	Kaplan Harris
Matthew Henriksen	Nick Comilla	Gregory Laynor
David McConnell	Jonny Leahan	Stephanie Young
Alan Bigelow	Skyler Dahan	Pierre Joris

Ben Hersey
Ngoc Doan
Marcella Duran
Angie Cat
Thomas Murphey
Dike Blair
Maged Zaher
William Tell
Sharon Mesmer
Steve Halle
Kendra Sullivan
Janyce Desiderio
Nicholas Gorham
Jenna Humphrey Wattenbarger
K. Lorraine Graham
Adam Kern
Marie Frignet des Préaux
John Thomas
Shaun Mader
Diane Greco Josefowicz
Emily Kendal Frey
Phil Kostov
Colton Brassie
Unlikely Stories
Simon Seapony
Mike Bailey-Gates
Andrea Crespo
Sharmila Cohen
Eddy Bird
Kim KymChi
Sally Laug
Mathias Svalina
Guillaume Morissette'
Mark Tursi
Angela Stubbs
Adrienne Walser
Daniela Olszewska
Andrew Mister
Aileen Saatchi
Ted Mathys
Susan Bee
N-Pop Eisenman
Gabrielle Calvocoressi
Chris Emslie
Lee Ann Brown
Cara Benson
Nate Pritts
Shaun Allen Mahan
Caryl Pagel
Polly Bresnick
Lynn Behrendt

Anna Swann-Pye
Izzy Tuason
Jesse Seldess
Sheppard R. Pepper
Stephanie Strickland
Andrew Klobucar
Zach Blas
Sara Wintz
Zhanna Chausovskaya
Matthew Needleman
Filip Marinovich
Bill Cohen Tatoosday
Jeff T. Johnson
Rachel Blau DuPlessis
Jasmine Washington
Sanchi Illuri
Marisa Crawford
Ray DeJesús
Jason Jimenez
Vanessa Blakeslee
Anne Waldman
Mackenzie Levitan
Darren Pasha
Katie Bondy
Bruce Covey
Simone White
Mia Bruner
Amy Moor
Rosanne Wasserman
Christian Bök
Jen Benka
Steve Benson
Michael Brodek
Lucas Hunt
Jamelle Gestwicki
Adam Marston
Christophe Le Fou
Jesse Kessel
Leigh Toast
Elizabeth Willis
Chris McCreary
Kyle Valenta
Andrew Joshua Stetson
Parrillo
John Beer
Maitri Mehta
Maria Caridad Alison
Lucio-Zwieback
Marthe Reed
Haugen Anton
Khenrap Yeshi

Ronaldo Wilson
Drew Cortrite
Patrick Carroll
Tristan Shepherd
Hallie Sekoff
Lumi Tan
Dara Wier
Jenny Guo
Liz Whitcomb
Ben White
Julia Borden
Jordan Eagles
Joyce Lainé
Ryan Collins
Kevin Champouz
Max Kessler
Will Anderson
Emma Smith-Stevens
Star Black
Patrick Culliton
Leo Gugu
Mike Luxemburg
Michael Klein
Adam Wilkinson
Nick Glastonbury
Greg Purcell
Homer J Shew
Brian Foley
Nicole Nyhan
Nicholas Jordan
Alban Fischer
Jay Danielewicz
Christian Salazar
Ned Moor
Hanna Andrews
Joanna Fuhrman
Cecily Iddings
Camilo Roldàn
Quintan Ana Wikswo
Penn Chan
Joanna Maharaj
Charlie Huisken
Sarah Parr
Jay Varner
Grace Miceli
Carter Halbrooks
Julien T. Hamon
Elissa Lewis
Max Pearl
Soren Stockman
Robbie PeTrov

Lizzy Green
Rebecca Rom-Frank
Fitz Fitzgerald
Lizzie Feidelson
Megan Coates Parsons
Mitch Swenson
Sofia Theodore-Pierce
Gena Kowalski
Jenna Halladay Gruer
Austin Buben
Farrah Field
Jennifer-Leigh Oprihory
Melanie Neilson
David Estornell
Caleb Hamby
Mg Roberts
Bethany Ides
Jennifer Manzano
Benjamin Hale
Micki Walsh Strawinski
Gale Dulev
Kate Angus
Joe Gillis
Dave Morice
David J Durbin
Gino Branciforte
Amalia Ulman
Sommer Browning
Rj Equality Ingram
Ariel Yotive
Terri Witek
Milton Morris
Marie Myman
Manu Del Peschio
Ana Lieberman
Nina Quirk-Goldblatt
John Jay Mottola Loonam
Mäy 'bellgreen
Anar Parikh
Benjamin Phillips
Liana Mitlyng Day
Alex Thomas Cavell Batkin
Julia Gittes
Rebecca Hutcheson
Roland Schwartz
Zachary Taube
Rebecca Rrickman
Harry Stecopoulos
Andrea Ricci
Mike Hauser
Zach Literally

Jocelyn Saidenberg
Mary Weston
Christina Davis
Godsjudgment Iscoming
Jake Moore
Mariann Colonna
Christine Pfister
Rebekah Latour
Jonathan Ehrenberg
Emily Kennard
Heather Scott Durbin
Loire Martin
Molly Pearlstein
Drew Charles Kalbach
Charlie Kuder
Joe Milford
Madline Elledge
Ashley Grier
Erin Weeks
Michael Roberts
Nelle Oh
Bj Randolph
Cody Elizabeth Buchanan
Ken Alexander White
Jason Thomas McCain
Kelsey Allagood
Austin Gresham
Noelle Armstrong
Colin Whelehan
Susanna Parrish
William Louis Smith
Hannah Stuart Lathan
Neha R Parthasarathy
Megan Hicks
DJ Cheek
Aaron Nicholas
Timothy Dallas
Kaya Zakrzewska
Kirk Bromley
Harry Burke
Parker Tettleton
Eve Alpert
Brandon Reddell
Steve Orth
Samantha Giles
David Carlson
Cole Heinowitz
Mark Franks
Laura Moriarty
Ji Yoon Lee
Carley Moore

Simon Taylor
Tina Wise Halter
Joel Allegretti
Iris Xu
Stephanie Mae Bachmann
Samuel Ace
Christian DeFonte
Eric Mohrman
Carrie Hunter
Beverly Pérez Rego
Valentin Schmitt
Janet Hamill
Bhanu Jacasta Kapil
Sandra-Ben Doller
Michael Gottlieb
Pattie McCarthy
Daniel Alexander
Anna Joy Springer
Andre Anderson
Christie Gilson
Carmen Canton
Abigail Child
Kateri Lanthier
João Meireles
Amanda Scala
Tyrone Williams
Noelle Kocot
Dawn Tripp
Madeline Gins
John Coletti
Lee Ann Brown
Mimi Gross
Adam Baran
Pam Lloyd
Stanley Frank
Mark Campbell
Mary Azure Reed
Counterpath Press
Martine Bellen
Brandon Barber
Corey Zeller
Flavio Caamaña
Louis Negin
Arrow As Aarow
Sam Lohmann
Norman Belk
Haley Rene Thompson
Amanda Loopz Maldonado
Joe Strummer
Ava Lehrer
Robert Cunningham

David Butt
Chi Dynasty
Jules Sothauskas
Carl Kelleher
Elaine Equi
Ben Kopel
Jessica O Marsh
Still Mgazin
Sarah Resnick
Lori Spruce
Sarah Certa
Dave Ross
Michael Pagan
Alessandro Gasparini
Allyson Paty
Paul Dressler
Trinie Dalton
Xanadude Loftparty
Roddy Schrock
Juan Pablo Montoya
Sarah Perks
Matthea Harvey
Rob Dupea
Michael Phillip Geffner
Daniel Moore
Susan Berger-Jones
Stonecutter Journal
June Ward
William Beecher
Maria Guggenbiuchler
Kyle Nabors
Turner Roth
Trevor Allen
Jen Bervin
Ilk Journal
Bridge Journal
Salt Hill Journal
Bodii Actualized
Ridhima Goyal
Tommy Moma
Punk Hostage
Abraham Avnisan
Subito Press
Rubens Akira Kuana
YesYes Bøøs
Zachary Paul
Envoyenterprises Les
Cave Canem
Michael Nardone
Brian Evenson
Sarah Rose

Seth Oelbaum
Gabby Bess
Diana Arterian
Rob Schlegel
LaTurbo Avedon
Frances LeMoine
Shabby Doll House
Ziggy Black
Rosana Zarza-Canova
Jehle Kae Keilana
Natalie McDirt
Macie Gransion
Jugsy Green
Jared Stanley
Daphne Sumtimez
Two Serious Ladies
Angela Nelthorpe
Larry Eigner's Biography
CouCou Poetry
Leftfield On Ludlow
Sarah Mariee Mclaughlin
Notemuy Wandee
Melanie Hubbard
William Allegrezza
Martin Dee II
Barrett Wolfe
Boost House
Brand Troemel
Andrew Maranzanor
Britney Rivers
Ziggy Boy Black
Dave Morice
Ezra Miller
Ishmael Klein
Gryphon Rue
Ann Lipscomb
Publia Pigeon
Saudale Review
Tasha Friedman
Kevin Barrett Weil
Elizabeth Bentley
Susie Timmons
Words As Works
Mike Wilensky
Juan Antonio Olivares
Commie Cluster

Eileen Maxson

Tara Maxson
Garret Smith
Andrea Neel
Karin Sandberg
Erwin Kho
Max Ockborn
Maartje Aben
Anjali Gupta
Sally Harley Silvestro
Laurel Goshinski
Ben Kingsley
Kelly Feagins Maxson
Lena Bergendahl
Noreen Maxson
Amy McDowell
Jan Descartes
Vinod Hopson
Andy Lynes
Rachael Morrison
Arie Bouman
Fumiko Ladd Chino
Laura Lark
Russel Etchen
Andrea Grover
Denis Maxson
Olivia Ciummo
Jezze Hulzer
Jon Rubin
Nicholas Calcott
Jenny Stark
Orvokki Halme
Allison Wiese
Maria Guzman Capron
Skip Elsheimer
Delaney HF
Jerstin Crosby
Amy Gironda
Matt Barton
David Wrangler
Anderson Wrangle
Jennifer Wan Santillan
Kathleen Amshoff
Lauren F Adams
Spencer Longo
Bree Edwards
Michael Kontopoulos
Amisha Gadani
Nick Pozek
Jacob Ciocci
Giana Marie Gambino
Michelle Fried

A Lizzi Jo
Mercedes Perez
Amos Levy
Mikey McParlane
Katie Mitchell
Sebastian Forray
David Wilcox
Dan Letson
Ivan Lozano
AJ Liberto
Josh Atlas
Tria Wood
Cody Ledvina
Terry Boyd
Al Eckstue
Rene Magdaleno
Maria Mangano
Bum Lee
Diana Gerlein
Jenny Conte
Joey Hays
Adam Allstar Blanton
Adriana Perez
Nick Fox-Gieg
Michael Pisano
Thomas Sturgill
Tiffany Sum
Benjamin Rosenthal
Dusti Rhodes
Laura Miller
Derk Wolmuth
Lauren Faigeles
Leslie Cervantez
Shana Moulton
John Peña
Boby Bigwitz
David W Halsell
Kathryn Sitter
Jason Colburn
Sean Morrissey Carroll
Robert Kollar
Casey Michele Luna
Patrick Phipps
Diane Barber
Takehito Etani
Michael K Taylor
Ally Reeves
Be Ve
Margaret Cox
Gregory Witt
Jon Beckley

Jody Hughes
David Jameson
Carolyn Lambert
Ariane Roesch
Matthew Tantillo
Daniel Eugene Fabian
Sean Mcmanus
Joe Ross
Claire Chauvin
Louise Chan
Nancy Douthey
Ben Bigelow
Hollye K Young
Bruce Colwell
Frank Rose
Brian Brown
Hilary Harp
Cassandra C. Jones-Jorgenson
Cheyanne Ramos Forray
Jenn Gooch
Guunhildur Una Jonsdottir
Jonathan Minard
Ian Ingram
Cbeau Jordon
Dandridge Reed
Mitchell Center
Odalis Chaćon
Claire Hoch
Jessica Rios
Stephanie Armbruster
Devon Britt-Darby
Teresa O'Connor
Adrian Page
Eric Sloss
Emily Trof
Scott Calhoun
John Sanderson
Rachel Stewart
Margherite Mickie Mirra Harley
Michael Strahan
Mariana At AvantGarden
Tha Brandon
Jessica Langley
Thomas Beard
Rene Cruz
Eva Linderman
Emina Gündüz
Jennifer Ward
Mary Magsamen
Keri Oldham
Charles Kevin Moore

J. Michael Hamilton
Paul Slocum
Rachel De Joode
Michael Bise
Julia Oldham
Ted Conway
Siobhán Tattan
Richard Bott
Sarrita Hunn
Marie Aly
Stacy Kehoe
Brett Kashmere
Esiri Erheriene-Essi
Seth Capron
Brian L. Frye
Roger Beebe
Blinky Yao
Jake Peterson
Peter Van Hynin
Lane Hagood
Suzie Silver
Fred M. Miller
Astria Suparak
Dennis Nance
Judith Schroiff
Jesse McLean
Annegret Kellner
Sarah Fenoglio
Carlos Vela-Prado
Emily Ng Little
Luke Luke
Jason Eitelbach
Woohoo Juliacks
Claudia Cortinez
Justin Ross
Matthew McKibben
Sandra Rodriguez
Kevin Mcgarry
Katie Kline
Wendy Vogel
Jade Yumang
Jessiza Tankard
Jahje Bath Ives
Sam Trussell
Eric Hester
Melissa Rourke
Jessica Ross
Leona Scull-Hons
Paoloma Polo
Jon Rafman
Rachel Valinsky

Éloïse Larochelle
Travis Lynn
Rory Pi
Golan Levin
Dean Terry
Jennet Thomas
Scott Andrew
Vanessa Haroutunian
Anne Angyal
Brian Satterwhite
Nibu Abraham
Jose Solis
Tijana Mišković
Alex Jacobs
Adrian Lama
Carrie Murphy
Lauren Cornell
Miloš Trakilović
Magnus Monfeldt
Martin Ivy
Alex Nguyen
Debbie Riddle
Jiajia Zhang
Brent Owens
Alex Dordoy
Mark R. Yzaguirre
Marisa Olson
Sarah De Vos
Libby Pratt
Elizabeth Thomas
Angela Fraleigh
Raed Yassin
Casandra Kellogg Noack
Jasmijn Visser
Archer D Midland
Hilary Wilser
Zachariah Durr
Cara Erskine
Lauren Reid
T.J. Dubz
Katrina Moorhead
Patrick Kwiatkowski
Nick Meriwether
William E. Jones
Michael Jones McKean
Sterling Allen
Darrin Martin
Jason Singleton
Christopher Shields
Sabine Ruitenbeek
Kim Van De Veerdonk

Willem de Rooij
Harald Den Breejen
Markus Cone
Erica Farrell
Rachel Cook
Lambros Papanikolatos
Mike Lyden
Jodi Moore
Bryan Zanisnik
Carlos Rosales-Silva
Bettina Johae
Claudia Solis
Martin van Zomeren
Wieske Wester
Kim Abshere
Lisa Pesak
Sylvie Fortin
Katja Mater
Evan DiLauro
Elizabeth Dunbar
Alexander De Lucena
Cheryl Moody
Fran Ledonio Flaherty
Marien Schouten
Mark Horn
Jeremiah Jones
Sarah Gish
Neave Casey
Heather Kelley
Matt McCormicj
Kelly Klassmeyer
Ted Passon
Alejandro Jimenez
Cory Arcangel
Coen Vunderink
Romain Loâzo
Koen Nutters
Allen Hendriz
Mckay Otto
Tobias Nilsson
Naomi Uman
Scott Peveto
Nico Feragnoli
Spencer Parsons
Chris Lockwood
John Carrithers
Thiago Hersan
Ed Halter
Fereshteh HT
Jill Pangallo
Kia Neill

Paul Mpagi Sepuya	Ginta Tinte	Rachel Hewlett
Melissa Hung	Suzanne Wallinga	Matthew Silver
J. Michael Stovall	Jack Holden	Jessice MilNeil
Pablo de Ocampo	Michele Yu	Churchill Willis
Katherine McCollough	Helene Lundbye Petersen	Jonathan Read
Yzaguire	Julia Halperin	Bucky Thuerwachter
Melissa Ragona	Nobutaka Aozaki	Judy Kwon
James Hays	Tyler Sutton	Judy Tedford Deaton
Jessie Stead	Baseera Khan	Mary Kuntz
Kim Beck	Maaike Gottschal	Lora Reynolds
Susan Venus	Ross Paterson	Jim Fetterley
William Betts	Raúl Diaz Reyes	David Wightman
Dean DeMatteis	Vincent Vulsma	Patricia Hernandez
Sohrab Kashani	Sam Ackerman	Austin Video Bee
Jarno Burger	Jason Cortlund	Michelle Illuminato
James Gandhi Range	Camilo Gonzalez	Eric Fleischauer
Mazine Kopsa	Conny Kuilboer	Sixto Wagan
Renske Janssen	Christopher Sperandio	Heather Illingworth Brogan
Zach McDonald	Thorey Mjallhvit	Niels Vis
Shmirit Malul	Martha Colburn	Theresa Halsell
Marlene Picard	Elizabeth White	Heidi Fabian
Avi Krispin	Jenny Schlief Morgan	Cynthia Toles
Lisa Ramsey	Corine Linderbegh	Chrs Martgenson
Jim Finn	Arturo Palacios	Shaun Jensen
Andrew Strasser	Dana Friis-Hansen	Indiana Audunsdottir
Zach Moser	Kendra Gaeta	Seth Mittag
Lucie Draai	Maclean Smyth	Lillian Warren
Melissa Hammesfahr	Mercedes Azpilicueta	Christopher French
Sorcha Landau	Joakim Drescher	Mary Maxson
Valerie Cassel Olivier	Robert Pruitt	Brittany Mariel Hudak
Matt Lipson	Rachel Blackney Tepper	Chris Jalomo
Laurence Miller	Mike Harley	Tish Anonimouse
Bryan Wendorf	Susanne Slavick	Bas de Boer
Andy Taylor	Kelly McDevitt	Matthew Landry
Sara Von Der Heide	Nicky Nikkels	Nele Vos
Romy Scheroder	Savannah Schroll Guz	Lori Alexander Lockerd
Andrew ebman	Constant Dullaart	Paul Hadley
Kelly Pike	Bill Davenport	Jenn Brehm
Dean Brandt	Stefan Ruitenbeek	Xochi Solis
Marion Verboom	Jennifer Schmidt	Fred Miller
Sands Murray-Wasisnk	Rainey Hudson	Lee Walker
Tamar Spook	Feiko Beckers	Lisa Qualls-Artist
Alfred Cervantes	Ambulantic Videoworks	Angela Grace Russell
Kristian Salinas	Levan Amashukeli	Kristin Miller
Melissa Berry	Ben Kruisdijk	Michele Kopycinski Kleeman
Sasha Dela	Enid Baxter Ryce	Amy Kopycinski Bodie
Nathan Green	James Duesing	Michi MatterJiigarjian
Sue Graze	Mike McAloon	Heiko Räpple
Molly Gochman	Brian Piana	Daile Janssen
Lynne McCabe	Thaddeus Kellstadt	Felipe Rizzo Prux
Caspar Stracke	Margarita Cabrera	Vicki Fowler

Ruth Campau
Mike Kupka
Kevin Moore
Rachel Hecker
Troy Schulze
Rachelle Vasquez
Annabella Cuomo
Star Massing
Diana Sofia
Carlos Lama
Sean Bradley
Maryellen Maxson Kline
Corkey Sinks
Johnny P. Thomas
Mike Shannon
Tha Joanna
Simona da Pozzo
Risa Puleo
Callen M
Pim Blokker
Belinda Hall
Brett Scieszka
Tom Harley
Todd Eacrett
Sengelmann Hall
Logan Sebastian Beck
Si Simona
Liv Strand
Stephanie Martz
Philip Pearlstein
Katherine Talcott
Tha ArtSalon
André Avelãs
Deborah Davidovits
Anais Moreaux
James Hill
Christian Friedrich
Chelby King
Annemieke Bouman
Bunnith Thok
Sidyon Cucaro
Delicia Harvey
Noa Giniger
Drew Martin
Joelle Dennis
Felix van der Hagen
Hannah Page Peacock
David Jablonowski
Mapping Place
Michelle Omichael
Hayley Williams Parks

Elisa Barry Smith
James Fotopoulos Fantasma
Julie Kinzelman
Sean Rudolph
Dolly Frances
Nick Hallett
Melange Creperie
Johanna de Schipper
Stephen Paul Heller
Prince Abdul Awal
Sarah Jane
Make Catopia Real
Patricia Bella-Gillen
Va Vaa
Christian Henkel
Jim Jennings
Zilm Jeff
Sarika Goulatia
Cinemad Presents
Sjoerd Oudman
Oreoo Gooaat
Lance Scott Walker
Matt Stilt
Paul Tarrago
Dev Cato
Florian Schroiff
Jason Abillama-Villegas
Gretchen Skogerson
Sonja Lowrey Zilm
Sara Schuh
Interstate BK
Jonathan Williamson
Carl Johan Högberg

Aiden Morse

Miles Davis-Kielar
Heiko Julien
Shawn Bradford
Arjun Ram Srivatsa
Jesse Darling
Jane Tobin
Joshua Citarella
Michael Staniak
Bunny Rogers
Dee Morse
Evan Drolet Cook
Bronte Hainsworth
Hamishi Jama Farah
Joseph Frederick Flynn
Anna Crews
Thomas Payne
Will Neibergall
Parker Ito
Brad Troemel
Joe Hamilton
Spike Snell
Josh Rowe
Sean Joseph Patrick Carney
Maffew Linde
Cody Williams
Matthew Landry
Lauren Dunn
Pip Archer
Jon Rafman
Andrew Underscore Read
Lucinda Florence
Sway Press
Taj Bourgeois
Zach Rhodes
Jack Fischer
Andy Bradin
Ry David Bradley
Nick Faust
Kat Herine
Byron Degen
Mitch Posada
Isaac Is Massive
Rui Alves
Darcy O'Loughlin
Megan Hanson
Kim Laughton
Shi Buffalo
Alexa Gould-Kavet
Marian Tubbs

Hella Trol Buzy
Lochsley Wilson
Martika Palmer
Scott Newman
Stephen Forsyth
Clint Oolong
Steve Lewer
Valentin Amossé
Blake Andrews
Tom Butler
Øs Crunc Teslà
Nathan Gillam
Jasper Spicero
Annelies Doecke
Penny Goring
Racquel Thow
Matto Lucas
Marine Marbleindex
Daniel longo
Sean Joshua Mikes
Andrea Crespo
Saul Appelbaum
Robbie Brannigan
Luke Van de Elzen
Liam Vaugha
Anna Johnson
Coão Jarlos
Helene Acosta
Tom Brooke
Rosey Diamond Marzella
Manuel Carvalho
Zoey Lee
Tori Day
Aishwarya Sudhakaran
Zak Krevitt
Ben Burgess
George Dandolo
Holly Craig
Will Nicolson
Jose Castillo Pazos
Felix Colgrave
Jonathan Tagasa
Jim Coulson
Matthieu Adamczyk
Elias Benardout
Caleb 'Llama' Dunn
Harry Crocker
Chloe Badcock
Pilot Chmielarczyk
Derek Paul Boyle
Willem Jakub

Bronte McVeity
Leah Woodberry
Tiarna George Dolliver
Geoff Dobson
Christopher Schreck
Damien Maloney
Corwin Peck
Ryder Ripps
Laura Wilson
James Ottaway
Daniel McCoy
Jonny Marchand
Lisa McPhee
Ora Arroyo López
Selina Tang
Louise Phillips
Leah Beeferman
Bryce Roney
Nicholaus Goossen
Aisling Hinchey
Caleb Yaxley
Lauren Helena May
Pelc-McArthur
Charlie Reynolds
James Bowen
Loïq Sutter
Rachel Valinsky
Lauren Turale
Jordan Tammens
Tom Hall
Jade Foster
Cecelia Charlotte
Giuliana Cornier
James Lucas
Luis Dante Fantarella
ʎǝʞoɿ ʎǝʞoɿ
Ben Knight
Jem Emery
Yandell Walton
Corey Heard
Courtney Harries
Kate Hambleton
Meg Chellis
Bradley Cannan
Megen Mary Fallon
Kenji Mc'Loughlin
Phoebe Cahill
Louisa Rebellato
Belinda Williams
Josh Rae
Reanne Chidiac

Leesa Greig
Beth Brownrigg
Louie Payne
Nick Perillo
Alex Grant
Joseph Griggs
Wendy Figueroa
Morgan Smith
Tayla Appleby
Matilda Brown
Stephen Davis-cook
Kathryn Whiteley
Julian Lambert
Rosie Savage
Gary Wilson
Thomas Holley
Beach Sloth
Emily Devlin
Tessa Frewin
Charles McCurry
Jane Rawlings
Lauren Sims
Amy Courto
Kim Asendorf
Joanne Degen
Jenn Bozoky
Lucille Bone
Patrick Reid
Brendan Scot Tidesley
Kimberley Bos
Jakob Barrett
Macaylah Morse
Tom McNamara
Jessica Holmes
Emily Kozak
Sarah Cardenzana
Bella Anna-rose Kenzie
Elke Jemima McVeity
Lachlan 'Scotty' McCall
Helen Munro
Hadi FallahPisheh
Alana R Kingston
Milly Coulson
Liberty Nash
Power House-Gallery
Hayley Chamberlain
Scott Arnott
Raymond Rojas López
Katrina Rose
Katariina Kovanen
Nick Corcoran

Taylor Johnston
Adam Akam
Alexi Bouras
Wolfgang Glowacki-Photography
Mike Lamey
Chelsea Violet
Kelly White
Declan Edwards
Kaleb Curran
Henry EggsnBacon
Corey Davis
Ravi Dharad
Jayke Brown
Art Crime
Olivia Stolp
Hayden Kleinman
Jackie Dixon
Harrison Hayes
Emily Devlin
Leeya Maingay
Jess Gall
Johny Crystal
Katrina Rose
Woodworks Framing
Katherine Smith
Bradley French
Kaerutan Kilmer
Evan Phoenix Kent
Beatrix Theadog
Tiarna Dolliver
Colton Fordyce
Nina Daniel
Jerrett Morrison

Wyatt Niehaus

Jamillah James
James Michael Shaeffer Jr.
Dana Ward
Dora Budor
Charlie Smith
Nick Faust
Sydney Shen
Nicole Reber
Lauren Christiansen
Chris Partridge
Andrew Norman Wilson
Joshua Citarella
Keith J. Varadi
Louis Doulas
Marisa Olson
James La Marre
Brad Troemel
Haley Mellin
Camille Bertrand
Artie Vierkand
Travess Smalley
Abby Rae Cornelius
Jamie Sterns
Jaakko Pallasvuo
Nancy Pants
Parker Ito
Johnny Tragedy
Rachel Fleischer
Alex Ross
Aaron Walker
Will Henry
Kevin Bruce
Andrew Christopher Green
Nick Pittroff
Ryan Lauderdale
Giampaolo Bianconi
Spencer Longo
Jack Dupp
Dan Baum
Gordon Hall
Nick DeMarco
Michael Manning
Crispin Best
Justin Kemp
Daniel Keller
Colin Edwin Statler
Colby Steele
Rick Herron
Débora Delmar
Billie Lee Francis
Chelsea Baker

Thor Shannon
Zach Blas
Theodore Darst
Shayna Brankamp
Jarrod Turner
Michelle RJ Rotuno-Johnson
Devin Kenny
Ciara Riddle
Andrew Birk
Sam Dwyer
Chris Reeves
John Knight
Zac Bailey
Rachael Milton
Kim Paice
John Rich
Gene McHugh
Daniel Everett
Lucy Chinen
Jon Konkol
Marco Rosso
Logan Niehaus
Deanna Havas
Matthew Rappo
Brian Droitcour
Eric Ruschman
Eli Mock
Iain Ball
Jimmy Fuentes
Toke Nielsen
Kristin Nsfw Doowllams
Ryan Lyle
Allisonrob Tanner
Marita Hergert
Matty Gaffney
Brianne Cain
Rasmus Emanuel Svensson
Karen Archey
Raven Howell
Chris Simmons
Nick Norton
Jacob Gaboury
Joe Hamilton
Sam McKinniss
Tiril Hasselknippe
Bea Fremderman
Joe Kay
Keith Schomaker
Daniel Quiles
Laura Brown
Alex York

Craig Moyer
Jesse Stecklow
Jamie Muenzer
Michael Ray-Von
Stefan Kalmár
Ryan Mulligan
Emily Ann Crabill
Charles Hyden
Blake Hardy
Joel Holmberg
Travis Jeppesen
Sebastian Botzow
Lilia Walsh
Riley Evans
Pete Fosco
Jack Schneider
Nina Chidichimo
Caitlin Robinson
Whit Buck VII
Anjali Alm-Basu
Carson Fisk-Vittori
Chris Chollins
Johannes Thumfart
Andrea Kaiser
Zachary Rawe
Riley Harmon
Andre Alves
Tasha Martin
Thorne Brandt
Juliette Bonneviot
Vincent Charlebois
Eugene Kotluarenko
Benjamin Bratton
Stephen Harris
Anthony Amrein
Katja Novitskova
Laurel Schwulst
Desmond Dale
Ryan Santos
Sally Glass
Arjun Ram Srivatsa
Brittany Skelton
Isaac Hand
Ella Plevin
Hannah Levy
Andrea Crespo
Tim Gentles
Kaela Noel
John Houck
Lydia Ewbank
Jimmy Swill

Christopher Schreck
Jacon Carson
Ann Hirsch
Jasmine Nicholas
Avril Thurman
Evan Drolet Cook
Santiago Taccetti
Harry Griffin
Susan Loftin
Martin Kohout
Joshua Jameson
Kachine Alina Moore
Jodie Cavalier
Allyson Duncan
Nathan Turner
Alex Peverett
Emma Creech
Aaron Graham
Annie Doran
Justine Ludwig
Robin Peckham
Yasi Ghanbari
Paul Coors
Max Pearl
Maggie Paxton
James Early
Caleb F Doughty
Anthony Antonellis
Ethan Riddle
Travis Hallenbecj
Rodanny Gee
Robert Beatty
Miyö Van Stenis
Niko Princen
Ceci Moss
Zachary Copfer
Daniel G. Baird
Jack Josephn Kahn
Annie Witte
Allison Buechelrode
Rebecca LaMarre
Eric Fleischauer
Peyton Dabney Copes
Jack Ramunni
Masoon Kamandy
Carson Chan
Arielle Emberson
Daniel Wallace
Denise Burge
Olivia Erlanger
Jeremiah Johnson

Steve Bishop
Todd Uttley
Catherin Stein
Rachel De Joode
Rebecca R Peel
Will Brand
David Dao Ellena
Tiara Chambers
Vienne Chan
Julie Grosche
Melissa Sachs
John Auer
Olivia Hamilton
McKenzie Wark
Brett Ginsburg
Steve Roggenbuck
Michelle Ulmer
Andrea Sisson
John A Niehaus
Bryan Patrick Swayze
Parkhurst
Ryan Estep
Aay Preston-Myint
Jason Schiedel
Yuri Pattison
No Marie
Asher Penn
Gavin Mueller
Gabriel Molnar
Enrico Boccioletti
Ali Hiba
Fabrizio Affronti
Miguel Morte Valentine
Loraine Wible
Michael Jones McKean
Vincent Uribe
Eddy Kwon
Weingrüll Karlsruhe
Nate Hitchcock
Joe Lamb
Amalia Ullman
Jeff Baij
Brian Uhl
Rosa Aiello
Adam Cruces
Chizzo Fo Rizzo
Tony Robertson
Cheon Lee
Megan Daley
Jacob Ciocci
Korakrit Arunanondchai

Paul Pieroni
Al Bedell
Steve Kemple
Jon Lorenz
Kevin Rubén Jacobs
Chris Mullins
Casey Kaplan
Daniel Rehn
Jessy Baum
Johnny Eudaly
Adam O'Reilly
Mauzy Virginia
Justin Wolf
John Michael Boling
Drew Flahery
Loney Abrams
Alice Charlotte Ray
Andy Marko
Eric Mack
Micah Schippa
Laura Fischer
Rick Silva
Huntr Muller
Monica Dick
Japes Christy
Ayn Teigman
James Gwynpll
Lindsay Howard
Si Swiss-Institute
Ryan J Hammoor
Bunny Rogers
Jasper Spicero
Ryan Poorman
Ken Katkin
Joshua Biehler
Jennifer Chan
Joe Speier
Alexandra Gorczynski
Dru Gerbel
Daif Kent
Evan Carroll
Nick Lalla
SongMing Ang
Ria Rogers
Gabbi Lanza
Julie Billter
Nick Scholl
Ché Zara Blomfield
Hadley Vogel
Lorena Conz
Maxime Guyon

Josh Pavlacky
Matt Morris
Danny Macovei
Kelly Frazier
Edward Marshall Shenk
Nic Disimile
Petra Cortright
Michelle Brenseke
Cisco Jimenez
Lorna Mills
Jasper Elings
Leah Fleischer
Sara Ludy
Emilie Gervais
Frederick Heydt
Ben Fly Sure
Todd McWhorter
Chelsea Ostrow
Rachel Fox
Perla Montelongo
Lacey Voss
Ricardo Domeneck
Melanie Bonajo
Frank Krugmann
Christopher Lefke
John Boyle-Singfield
Melissa Kasey
Lucy Fuller
Flemming Ove Bech
James Schenck
Lydia Rosenberg
Billy Rennekamp
Mark A. Fionda Jr.
Alex Mackin Dolan
Allison Young
Wyatt S. Routson
Amanda Kisor
Gregory Fong
Lauren Reid
Chelsea Rae Price
Ted Porter
Nine Yamamoto
Izzy Clark
Jenn Bacon Bauer
Sarah Min
Rollin Leonard
Colleen GlitterPrincess Celsor
Daniel Wickerham
Maximiliano Alejandro Zas
Shana Moulton

Guy Michael Davis
Elda Oreto
Mark Byron
Daap Galleries
Manuel Solano
Cheyenne Ohmer
Carrie Phillips
Gregor Rozanski
Christina Mauro
Sarah Shives
Joshua Abelow
Kareem Lotfy
Ilya Smirnov
Jónó Mí Ló
Kristin Tretheway
Jeremy Bailey
Stephen Thomas Sause
Ashley Walton
Kelsey Krekeler
Alexis L. Grisé
Chris Kulcsar
Spencer Sweeney
Lyndon Probst
Alfredo Salazar-Caro
Michelle Ceja
Sam Locey
Alix Ross
Zoë Salditch
Rick Jacobsen
Anne de Vries
Javier Peres
Chris Campbell
Kim Asendorf
Dan Wolff
Britta Thie
Marlous Borm
Ollie Hogan
Christopher Campbell
Manuel Fernández
Hunter Hunt-hendrix
C Spencer Yeh
Jordan Tate
Lawrence Kumpf
Andrew Russeth
Angelo Plessas
Laurel Nakadate
Corwin Peck
Andrew Durbin
Piper Marshall
Liam Alfred Clark
Peter Ibsen

Domenico de Chirico
Colin Self
Dena Yago
Cleopatra's Greenpoint
Erin Rioux
Chris Kraus
Jon Cates
Patrick Cruz
Daniel Chew
Robert Wiegmann
Chadwick Gibson
Zachary Davis
Kevin Mcgarry
Rico J. Reyes
Max Schreier
Justin Ross
Thomas Macker
Paige Warman
Travis Fitzgerald
Laura Brothers
Jenny Yoo
Slava
Micaela Durand
Lorenzo Durantini
Robbie Fitzpatrick
Christopher Clubb
Alex Freedman
Guthrie Lonergan
Chris Bartell
Leah Dizon
Brett H. Isaacoff
Sherwin Rivera Tibayan
Adam Pettit
Tony Shumski
Adam Bech Harms
Tyler Wallace
John Erik Marshall
Marc Governanti
Patrick Lubon
Kelani Nichole
Sam Falls
David de Bol
Stephen Truax
Emily Robertson
Timur Si-Qin
John Transue
David Knowles
Joe Graham-Felsen
Erik H Rzepka
Kristen St. Clair
Yuyeon Cho

Jonathan Vingiano
Krist Wood
Minda Burton
Kristen Denier
Wii Winters
Dominic Quagliozzi
Lee Carraher
Andy Stroble
Zachary Kaplan
Derek Jon Scacchetti
Eric Wrenn
Jared Rosenacker
Joanna Osher
R.lord
Michael Mills
Louise Sharrow
Dylan K.H. Thomas
David DeWitt
Wade Lam
Alex Jameson
Melissa A Mewadows
Katie Wilson
Raymond Seyfried
Daniel Lawson
Erin Deters
Rachel Voelker
Rosie Kovacs
Paul Slifcak
Kate Wenderfer
Matt Shaw
Lynda C. Lucas
Molly E. Sullivan
Shelby Elizabeth
Brian Labus
Micah Freeman
Milan DelVecchio
Philip Spangler
Zachary Tyler
Calla Henkel
Karl Walker
Pete Ohs
Bradley Charles
Chris Thompson
Hunter Skye Chamberlain
L. Ren Hicks
Michael Douglas Rudi
Jane Bruce
Emiline Sites
Samantha Best
Behn Browne
Jeiko Julien

Lisa Tompkins
Heather Ouellette
Andrew Candels
Lizzy DuQuette
Jen Schroeder
Ryder Ripps
Krystal South
Michael Ruiz
Chase Whiteside
Joseph Boyd
Cab Broskoski
Sara Corley
Ryan Whittier Hale
Geneviève Belleveau
Michael Madrigali
Alana Celii
Jude Mc
Will Andrée
Jacolby Satterwhite
Dylan Fisher
Elise Thompson
Lawrence Lek
Lauren Altman
Ian Aleksander Adams
Alex Ebstein
Em DiRienzo
M Michael Smith
Mark Beasley
Leah Recht
Adam Longbonz
Esteban Schimpf
Sarah Whitwell
Michael David Quattlebaum Jr
Tabor Robak
Jake Dibeler
Damon Zucconi
Patricia Murphy
Amy Scarpello
Tara Downs
Sterling Crispin
Kari Altmann
Casey Jane Ellison
Jake Ellioitt
MacGregor Harp
Suzanne Lett
Aureliano Segundo
Hannah Billy
Brendon Miller
Jose Castillo Pazos
MayaLou Banatwala
Katelin Reeser

Josefer Sánchez
Robert Thomas Heppel
Mike Goldby
Jeanette Hayes
Floyd-From Ohio
Joe Korbee
Erica Lapadat-Janzen
Hayley Aviva Silverman
Molly Donnermeyer
Kate Sansom
Josh Botts
Zach Searcy
Dave Brott
Rachel Valinsky
John Goodpaster
Brandon Hawkins
Jason Huff
Gabrielle Antoine
Jill Roebel
Yesir Muhabin
Katie Torn
John Kilduff
Kyle Carpenter
Francisco Cordero-Oceguera
Dave Greber
Kelsey Koewler
Tony Chrenka
Nicolas Stefano Pedde Lay
Martin Cole
Mark Nelson
Jon Rafman
Matthew Flahery
Ni Na
Kristine Valentinsen
Basti Paulitzka
Érik Spínola
Solvej Helweg Ovesen
Cecca Lina Morrone
Spencer Hinson
Tony Granger
Despina Stokou
Jesse Darling
Justin Kelly
Tristan Klaus
Simon Denny
Samuele Papiro
Andy Licardi
Thomas Cheneseau
Deandre Moxley
Solomon Chàse
Tyler Los-Jones

Patrick Mclaughlin
Aleph Escobedo
Joseph Nicholson
Florent Delval
Annika Kuhlmann
Alma Alloro
Laure Devereaux
Holly Elizabeth Quinn
Joel Cook
Edmund Chia
Roy Ascott
Jason Metcalkf
Julian Haterskeeptalkinu-
makinm Foxworth
Olga Sureda
Asli Serbest
Fleur Van Dodewaard
Rhys Coren
Lauren Cornell
Troy Gallagher
Spring HongKong
Gloria Maria Cappelletti
Casey Nelson
Kat Anna Somody
Alby Maccarone
Carl Seffers
Joseph Yølk Chiocchi
Neil Morrow
Ilja Karilampi
Geronimo Cristobal
Aleksandra Domanović
Nadia Garb
Donna Huanca
Jon Satrom
Theodore Jackson
Christa Joo Hyun
D'Angelo
Blake Andrews
Aaron Harbour
Nebbie Loon
Caroline Dorsey
Marcel Alcalá
Mike Young
Hanna Nilsson
Organ Armani
Ry David Bradley
Nancy Leticia
Will Neibergall
Lauren Pascarella
Balthazar Berling
Brent Lashley

Dan Bodan
Heather Marie
Aye- AyeBooks
Jonah Porter
Patricia Ann Chal
Hannah Perry
Joe Fletche Orr
Lorenzo Benedetti
Bradford Kessler
Rózsa Zita Farkas
Elena Bajo
Torito Toro
Lyndsy Welgos
Caitlin Denny
Emilio Gomariz
Adam Sammons
Nadja Sayej
Eric Deller
Brian Kokoska
Michael Peacock
Emily Hackett
Dusty Stalcup
Liliana Lewicka
Charlotte Cheetham
Logan White
Jonas lund
Kasia Gumpert
Ben Elliot
Bryce Grates
Lauren Elder
Kenny Heidenreich
Derek Frech
Jessica Eaton
Paul Alexander O'Neil
Mitch Posada
Jack French
Franklin Melendez
Georges Jacotey
Raul de Nieves
Travis Pearce
Ed Halter
Kelly Reinaker
Jason Lazarus
Ross Warman
Pierre-Arnaud Doucède
Gregory Laynor
Sydney Wise
Jesus Javier
Simon Guzylack
Kenichi Matsumoto
Sofie Mariana

Sylvia Gutowska
Kenneth Wright
Jordan Wolfson
Ania Urbanski
Christina Klee Kilbane
Rosa Menkman
Janice T. Sunflower
Patrick Lichty
Andreas Meinich
Alice Hopkins
Kuby Nnamdie
Ross Iannatti
Brion Nuda Rosch
Maria LoBuono
Andrea Noce
Colton Brassie
Rebecca Salvadori
Amanda Ross-Ho
Ed Fornieles
Mula Broach ActBoy
Emilie Bok
Wojciech Kosma
Aude Pariset
Mike Bale
M Samuel White
Hans Eriksson
Ricky James
Grey Area
Domenico Quaranta
Johan Rosenmunth
David Cano
Thomas Raabe
Lisa Siders
David Caille
Nicolas Sassoon
Aron Gent
Rod Barton
Amitai Romm
Chiara Badinella
Dmitrij Maslovskij
Jon Feinstein
Daniel Temkin
Vvork Book
Michael Staniak
Jeff Knowlton
Evan Berberich
Jessie Hoffman
Kaja Cxzy Andersen
Emily Rose Cmar
Anabelle Arlie
A Bill Miller

Tim Donovan
Lucas Blalock
Marty Rossman
Alex Bunn
Samuel François
Sabrina Ratté
Brian Blomerth
Nate Boyce
Hhanne Mugaas
Saurabh Anand
Oswaldo Ruiz
Dorian Nicholas Grinspan
Pxvl Bxrsch
Steven Stewart
Peyton Piquard
Peter Kirn
Maja Cule
Constant Dullaart
Nicole Foran
Martijn Hendricks
Brooke Candy
Matthew Spencer
Sean Mink
Zachary Shay Hüber
Corinna Kirsch
Nathan Lee
Jimmy Baker
Helga Wretman
Adriana Ramić
Tom Weinrich
Roy Avital
Michiel Ceulers
Indira Aguilera Kohl
Skylyn Lee Ohlenkamp
Jamar Larkins
Sarah Brunner
Alex Hatch
Jay Danielewicz
Erik can der Weijde
Derek Ruch
Ben Foch
Marion Patricia
Jesse A Greenberg
Helen Ad
Terence Hammonds
Jake Conner
Guillaume Maraud
Janus Høm
Kyle Burns
Brian Khek
Tyrell Pentz

Ben Kleesattel
Giselle Zatonyl
Gary Jayne-Whatever
Evan Lenox
Stephanie Janet Nagel
Ry Wharton
Rasmus Myrup
Bas Fisher Invitational
Christian Velasquez
Outpost Artists Resouces
Randall Slocum
Steve Turner
Sofia Leiby
Shane Mecklenburger
Yoshi Sodeoka
David Wightman
Jeremy Smith
Hunter Bradley
Joey Versoza
Eva Papamargariti
André Carlos Lenox-Samour
Katie Parker
Bryan Morello
Petros Moris
Joshua Montoya
Amadeo Kraupa-Ruskany
O Tannenbaum Berlin
Ignacio García
Mitchell Charbonneau
Art Damage
Andrew Cape
Kentaro Takaoka
Xavier Madrid
Lindsay Lawson
Maffew Linde
Jackson Xoxo
Sam Bates
Joe Syverson
Matt Starr
Johnathan Mclemore
Luis Albuquerque Pinho
Joe Meister
Courntey Hausfeld
Kelsey Kalnow
Tracy Schoenhoft
Sarah Marcella Casnellie
Natalie Lohr Meininger
Jake Fabrey
Mark Pieterson
Samuel D. York
Katie Ziegler

Alexanda Hananel
Manuel Buerger
Lindsey Dougherty
Bunk Spot
Nina Morris
Adrian Smith
Matthew Landry
Seán Denning
Samantha Brockfield
Marco Strappato
Jane Michell
Christopher Trimbach
Josh Kwang-Hee Lee
Drew Xavier Brockmeyer
Anthony Hemingway
Wayne Berg
Ryan Moster
Jamie Daly
Suzi Wood
Scott Starkey
Rebecca Zeiler
Ole Jannek
Grahm Jones
Megan Trimbach
Bradley Evans
Rob Pfister
Kevin Boeckman
Drew Baverman
Monica America PearTree
Neal Hartman
Danielle Nicole
Caitlin Janes
Mantha Norton
Anne Parker
Joe Mueller
Matthew Berens
Katerine Ascue
Randi Maxwell
Elizabeth Burkhart
Mary Neumann
Elizabeth Trantanella
Heather Kasdan
Filippo Berta
Dan Stiver
Tess Hackett
Holly Bird
Tim Jett
Kat Mills
Caleb Cornelius
Di Fang
Matei Samihaian

Myeongsoo Kim
Amanda Dunigan
Maria Lanko
Centre D'art Bastille
Alex Greggory
Francesco Cagnin
Mark Hanavan
Tiffany Bishop
Ivan Fucich
Martha Otero
Emanuel Rossetti
Omowaleola Omosebi
Mario Zoots
Rhulon Hart
Kernel Ops
Benjami Asam Kellogg
Galerie Jeanrochdard
Leah Stahl
Sophie Dougadir
Timothy Leslie
Michael D. Everett
Harry Burke
Raffaella La Vena
Stephan Tanbin Sastrawidjaja
Matt Murphy
Giuseppe Pinto
Nicki Davis
Drew Wheeler
Josh Hughes
Andrey Bogush
Lori Firestone Molfenter
Rossella Redbit
Carol Tyler
Ben Alper
Todd Herzog
Zach Kincaid
Stephan Backes
Tank london
Jean Follman
Genevieve Costello
Tatiana Leshkina
Seth Adelsberger
Michael Hymer
Brandon Reddell
Matt Castells
Michael Bell-Smith
Kim Corenlius
Quinn Keaveney
Jose Becerra
Charlie C C Audsley
Matt Hornung

Marvin De Deus
Heesuk Che
Brad Tinmouth
Ida Lehtonen
Supermassive Blackhole
Dylan Reid
Sarah Kitsinis
Scott Licardi
Brendan Bogosian
Yngve Holen
Andrew Rosinski
Piet Mondriaan
Dan Rees
Jamian Juliano-Villani
Nezhnaya Sariya
Felix AndMumford
Kate Moss
Mamli Shafahi
Skyler Schubert
Darian Dauterich
Fringe Arts Bath
Charlie Smith London
Lance Wakeling
Jack Gross
Dominik Podsiadly
Sparwasser Hq
Larissa Mischoff
Kate Wilson
Shawn C. Smith
Nogueras Blanchard
Tyler Dobson
Ethan Cook
Maria Seda-Reeder
Vito Modugno
Mockers Clubs
Saul Appelbaum
Enrico Centonze
James Miller
Judy Steele-Mitchell
Solace Fragment
Cory Richard Davolos
Manny Palou
Ryan Alexander
Bricks London
Glogauair Berlin
Mike Ziegler
Shelby Nungester
Francoise Gamma
Ed Varie
Priz Tats
Alex Israel

Philipp Otto
Hendrik Niefeld
Soundfair Berlin
Tim Berresheim
Nile Koetting
TransientProjects ToPeople
Theodoros Giannakis
Noise Praise
Jean-Philippe Ronnan
Hugo Scibetta
Agente Doble
Arthur Brum
Vulpes Vulpes London
Mike Daniels
Tanya Leighton
Arcadia Missa
Sarah Samy
Gsb Gsb
Inti Romero
Primitive London
HO PE
Nomas Rome
Latorretta Sulborrgo
Woww Mgzne
Jahvier Peretz
Black Tent Press
NewGallery London
Jessica Sanders
Anna Baverman
Bruce LaBruce
Sasha Kazantsev
Idgi Guy
New Young Leeds
Haydon Boss
Bristol Drawing-Club
Brenna Murphy
Centrum Berlin
Esteban Ottaso
Roy Hutchinson
Laura Stratton
Lali Foster
Ramon Alon
New Capital
Jon Nash
Debora Delmar Corp
Jonathan Mechail Caldwell
Richard Skyler
Jimmy Junk
Barcelona Showcase
Pootee Moore
Kamilia Kard

Art House Wakefield
Centre D'édition Contemporaine
Tasos Gaintatzis
TheBeardshop Hamburg
Kate YeonJeong An
Pro Numb
Fabio Santacroce
Leap Berlin
Bird Jpg
Ben Sid
Crescent Contemporary
Melissa Burns
Vasily Zaitsev
Pteron Press
Emiliano Aversa
Kïller Instïnct
BigGhost Fase
Mexico Projectspace
Simon Ulysses
Envoyenterprises Les
Meghan Morrow
Stroud Valleys Artspace
Tensta Konsthall
Shingo Tsubouchi
Khaled Galaleldeen
New Dennis Knopf
Anthony Stagg
Miner Pie
Sonja Lowrey Zilm
Lyonn Redd
Galerie Valentin
Ken Bruce
El Corbusier
Heimatmuseum London
Karam Jester
Mattie Hillick
Zilm Jeff
Chris Brown
A Black Jpeg
Mulford Tightner
Anton KernGallery
Index Stockholm
Storbjørn Cardán
Quire Elizabeth
Gently MrFrankly
Tool Shed Arts
Kombinat Literaturberlin
Dot Dot
Wes Noble
David Cope
AnagramBooks London

Disko Zap
Büro Egfk
Km Temporaer
Macie Gransion
Andy Familia Stroble
LaTurbo Avedon
Aggtelek Duo
Naomi Curd
Océane Picard
Greg Forst
Discovering Borderlands
Britney Rivers
Jonathan Chacón
Ton Awe
Morry Mathaway
Jenny Davis
Ben Fino-Radin
David Rickard's
Chris Coy
Antek Walczak
Avg Exorcist
Sarah Jane
Theo Contemprelics Ries
Štévèn Pàul Ščhàviń
Hunter Hughes
Selena Nabokov
Jake Swanson
Retrospective Hudson
Altes Finanzamt
NullandVoid Arts
Terasa Albert
Off Line Object
Interstate BK
Liz Goodman

Corwin Peck

April Fallarino
Beacon's Closet
Adam Katz Singing
Tan A. Lin
Dale W. Eisenger
Brad Troemel
Abigail Muir
Rachel Zeiger-Haag
Eric Burstyn
Colin Self
Yelene Soloveva
Mad Ask
Vernon Howl
Brendon David Mills
Taj Bourgeois
Holly Melgard
Tom Strangemint
Sophia Le Fraga
Matvei Yankelevich
Mark Baumer
Lionel Lamy
Dana Vaccarelli
James Peck
Joe Hamilton
Same Text
Ricky Carlson
Parker Ito
Michael Valinsky
Meg Ryan
Anne H. Keffer
Alanna Monet Carlson
Cory Rheault
Jenny Harris
Nicholas Inspektor Sodapop Ray
Kailtyn Hornblower
Tanya Pantene Harding
Alexa Carson
Lara Schiling
Steffy Yaryar
Anders Bergland
Matthew Goodrich
Murat Pulat
Ace McNamara
Darren Bader
Henriette Rønneberg
Oresti Tsonopoulos
Andrew Wilson
Mariana Lucia Orbay
Guy Weltchek
Lain Kay
Joe Waine

Joshua Citarella
Jessie Hu
Neal Burstyn
Louise Petersen
Austin Hays
Will Cole
Leah Evans
B. Colby Hamilton
Dave Greber
Sean Borman
Julia Popescu
Cindy Wheeler
Laura Leontine
Beaux Gestes Jezioranski
Andy Hadaway
Raul de Nieves
Diego Zucchini H
Amit Greenberg
Hamishi Jama Farah
Emma Griswold Stephens
Sandra Esther Ciriello
Eva Björg Hafsteinsdóttir
Evie Elman
Vanya Lombardi
Joey Frank
Alta Jeanine Finn
Allison Press
Onias Timothy Dickson
Megan Fuller
Jonathan Witt
Sylvia Jeffriess
Andrew Zawacki
Sarah Rothberg
Bunny Leopard
Mike Poste
Ryan Heyner
Tilman Hornig
Natasha Stagg
Aldís Rún Ingólfsdóttir
Kim Shirkhani
Alissa Adams
Nelson Yeo
Jessie DeStefano
Salad Prince Larry
Billy Crystal
Lacie Zassman
Lucy Wilson
Jason Sebastian Russo
Reese Lopez
Emily Wenner
Um Fa Gn

Nick Faust
Coco Mari
Nikki Bean Bristow
Kat Caban
Valerie Peck
Nathan DuToit
Anna Barie
Golden Fields
Cara Clinton
Sam Lohmann
Cade Beck
Austin Robey
Jasmine Ahrndt
Matthew Craven
Aisha Elizabeth
Jillian Peña
Mark Haslam
Charles Alexander
Anthony Don Z
Washti Windish
Ryder Ripps
Rachel Williams
Dana Suchow
Sara Calland
Johnny Simon
Noah Rabinowitz
Carly Rabalais
Chelsea Marks
Cameron Michel
Adam Radakovich
Ethan Cook
Robbie Kelley
Meagan Mari Gable
Jenny Correa
Tess Adele
Emily Ritchie
Ian R. McCarthy
Emily Wilson
Artie Vierkant
Josephus LaBier
Amanda Finn
jeff bowers
Casey Brewe
Öykü Tekten
Stephanie Williams
Nicky Tiso
Jon Koenig
Jeff Baij
Ilana Shulman
Todd Herres
Lucia Harmon

Josh Sargent
Sarah Kinlaw
De Se
Katarina Tarr
Steohanie Balascio-Koenig
Tal Isaac Hadad
Sir Kay
Karmella Fiebke
Michael C. Dumler
Andreas Beraha
Cameron Rheault
Amelie Ray
Ismar Masinovic
Sara Villard
Anthony Valdez
Beth Moon
Sara Taylor
Matthew Ryan Palmgren
Joshua Courtney
Sean A. Kasanova
Orrie Chazin
Megan Wang
Laura Fettig
Elizabeth Geeslin
Alex Williams
Shawn C. Anderson
Leonor Aispuro
Diana Tourjee
Vicki Peck
Andrew Hubing Evans
Drew Ramey
Ben Kay
Lilja Dögg Tryggvadóttir
Katie Waldeck
Ghazi Barakat
Natalie Reed
Alia Bistranin
David Fruchter
Tony Sodano
Kalen Olsn
Savannah Wyatt
YounJun Koo
Scott Young
Jaime Gleixner
David Wolach
Callan Clendenin
Jennifer Quillen
Leigh Alison Farrell
Kayla Andres
Brady Miller
Rob Fitterman

Bee Are
Daniil Kharms
Patrick Seeger
Caroline Yess
Joshua Madrid
Emma Quaytman
Aiden Morse
Christiana Key
Andrew McNey
Lance Holloway
Stephanie Rose
Aaron Derosso
Matt St. Gelais
Gordon F Cady
Justin McKnight
Alex Stewart
Brittany Asam
Kate Engelmann
Andrew Norman Wilson
Stephanie Reger Weitmann
Sean Thomas Blott
Sonia Stagg
Keren Richter
Samuel Draxler
Bryce McNichols
Wyndham Manning
Tara Zabor
Sarah Lipman
Alexandra Tatarsky
jacklyn grossfield
Shonna Gist
Erin Mulberg
Evan Klane
Unnameable Boox
Taryn Humphrey
Ann Hirsch
Jenna Thonander
Danielle Rose Nason
Christopher Ryan Larson
Petra Kleinlein
Cortney Taylor
Connor Haug
Alexandra Gorczynski
Matt Hendrickson
Rollin Leonard
Aashish Jethra
Mark Robinson
Chris Ryan
Derek Paul Boyle
Derek Galey
Ben Furman

Andrew Shubin
Ryan Evans
Persis Meowmeni
Kayla Andres
Martin F. Farrell Jr.
Judy Le
Trevis Peterson
Christy Shoff
Brian Work
Tim Williams
Kyle Thompson
Liza Kogan
Samanta Kaye Hart
Cole Janini
Matt Gearhart
Shari B
Ben Carson
Josh Santana
Will Carpenter
Buster Ross
Kate Siegel
Steve Weiler
Kim Hoppe
Kerry Farias
Blu Jean
William Owen
Sarelle Caicedo
Rookie Love
Eva Saunders
Paul Israel
Chanel Tomko
Nicholas Jackson
Robyn Adair
Ali Jopp
Natty Hagood
Rosie Math
Brooke Stepp
Tim Gage
Victor Sanders
Ma Sha
Erik Podhora
Andrew Olmsted
Sarah Crisp
Kenrick Ward
Riva Roller
Kelsey Locken
Elaine Palmer
Elizabeth Loewy
Ibiza Delaney
Cherie Burnett
Contessa Johnson

Claire Hanson
Courtney Zink
Matthew Louv
Holly Stanton
Snædis Sif Benediktsdóttir
Nola Barie
John Kim
Liam Goslett
Kayla Nichole
Rachel Valinsky
Cody Miller
Dustin Kimsey
Sean Monaghan
derek wawrzyniak
Emily Gruca
Ninfa Solorzano
Máni M Sigfússon
Johanna Gutierrez
Jon Rafman
Leona Renee Ross
Derek Folers
Sam Tarrel
Andrew Porter
Derek Goldenstein
Jennifer Parks
Trent DeBaere
Meghan McNealy
Bill Ross
Amy DeGiovanni
Kate Ryan
Joey Fitch
Sara Gates
Aldo D'Luna
Lennon Bergland
Josh Kline
Chris Sorensen
Vee J Lumpenprol
Oskar Peacock
Katie Gregg
Austin Stewart
Delcey Aislynn Flemming
Becca Taplin
Mr. President S.K.
Tori Covert
Ben Markus
Eric Leiser
Al Barb Brown
Charlene Bergland
Caity Bower
Jahn Hall
Matty Fasano

James Bowen
Eli Evans
Christine Hvidt Grønborg
Carolina Groensleth
Charlie Roman
Nick Benson
Brad Ray
JustinHoey
Yelena Niazyan
Rebecca Stewart
Catherine Grothus
Welby Alexander Gliszinski
Corrie Ferguson
Chelsea McCarthy
Johanna Marion Snell
Janice Rasmussen
Brandi Prewitt
Anna Izabela Bloda
Emily Beanblossom
Mike Law
Diane Alexis Dollar
Zakaria Raju
Brook Strong Bergland
Luke Brotherton
Roman Saliva
Amy Fine
Tatsuya Nyc
Maggie Heath
Stella Martin
Wyatt Niehaus
Suzanne VanBebber
Kelsey Klecker
Matt Falk
Ronnie LaGrone
Pierre Stone
Alexandra Hind
Jessi Cornett
Sam Roudman
Lauren Hunt
Darwin Eagleton
Errin Ferguson
Lily Ciccarone
Kat Danger Sawyer
Birth Beats
Jordan Tate
Logan Park
Trine Aarøe Torp
Joy Wolcott
Marshall Hicks
Sue Gold
Liz Hill

Spencer Taylor
Hadi FallahPisheh
Jeremy Markman
Krystal Brown
Livewithanimals Artspace
Jacki Rexford
Rick Moe
Matt Lyins
Alex Porta
Orion Russell
Tuff Town
Kassandra Havens
Emik Serna
Mandy Coletti
Emmy Wildwood
Windish Michel
Curriculum Vita
Vita Cat
Lyric Hunter
Jessica McCullough
Anna Crews

Jordan Tate

Riley Harmon	Marty Bode	Christie Brewer Boyd
Katie Parker	Nick Faust	Joe Lingeman
Joshua Citarella	Daap Galleries	Leah Dixon
Keith J. Varadi	Lauren Seiden	Carlos Tobar
Artie Verkant	Marcio Lopes	Sondra Meszaros
Dora Budor	Sean Bird	Hunter Jonakin
Colin Klimesh	Mark Slankard	Star Child
Rachel Fleischer	Kristopher Holland	Vann Geondeff
Lauren Christiansen	Jessica Parris Westbrook	Sim Luttin
Michelle Green Lopes	Maggie Wichman	Barry W Hughes
Fred Bidwell	Elizabeth Raymer Griffin	Joe Girandola
Brad Troemel	Jesse McLean	Marisa Zapata
James Michael Shaeffer Jr.	Andi Baumgartner	Rebecca Loyche
Marisa Olson	Gene McHugh	Rebecca Drolen
Ian Breidenbach	Elizabeth Denny	Jared Landberg
Rick Silva	Matt Griffin	Letha Wilson
Rachel De Joode	Jeff Baij	Ry Wharton
Louis Doulas	Bobby Scheidemann	Becky Foley
Alejandro Miguel Justino	Dylan Quirk	Bonnie Richardson
Crawford	Jessica Simorte	David P. McMillen
L.C. Tate	Anthony Antonellis	Luke Phillips
Neon Heater	Marty Rossman	Todd Herzog
Johannes Thumfart	Shelley Given	Ann Hirsch
Christy Wittmer	Rosemary Jesionowski	Arthur Liou
Anna Galt	Marc Horowitz	Aaron Steele
Phillip Schaefer	Justin Stafford	Ian Whitmore
Mike Kiniyalocts	Max Manning	Rich Vogel
Sterling Crispin	Caitlin Robinson	Eily Shoreder Willis
Daniel Keller	Noah Applebaum	Elizabeth Claffey
Aaron Hegert	Todd Nadenichek	Rachel Larsen
Manuel Buerger	Andrew Birk	Cliff Tierney
Joey Gomberg McNamee	Annie McNewney Tate	Christine Shank
Linda Ding	Andre Alves	Zach Kowalczyk
Jeremy Bailey	Sidney Ann	Caroline M LeFevre
Emily A. Paolucci	Shanka McGlotten	Ethan Riddle
Owen Mundy	Ian Horwtiz	Justine Ludwig
Justin Warrick	Philip Venables	Conor Backman
Stephanie Sadre-Orafai	Tim Methric	Duncan Smith
Justin Waddell	Mia Bird	Hillary Demmon
Guy Michael Davis	Isaac Bloom	Riva Jewell-Vitale
Kate Steciw	Rollin Leonard	Betsy Stirratt
Samantha Burns	Martin Guentert	Kristin Smith
Marni McFly	Jordan Bissett	Mike Miller
Lizzy Wagoner	Michael Manning	Brad Wicklund
Kelani Nichole	Andrew Norman Wilson	Jay Seawell
Ross Iannatti	Jeni Blacklock	Arthur Hash
Marco Rosichelli	Lindsey Godwin	Scotty Weddle
Tiffany Carbonneau	Leah Howell	Elaine Suzanne
Tiffany Dolder-Holland	Katja Novitskova	Chris Reeves
Jeremy Boyd	William Lamson	Adam Fithers
William Knipscher	Jason Zeh	Christina Allegree

Julie Long
Mia Dalglish
James Francis Flynn
Garrett Poortinga
Samuel York
Lauren Rentz
Sona Pastel-Daneshgar
Mathew A Powers
Jenny El-Shamy
Megan Strobel
Isabela Prado
Joy Usner
Ryan Mandell
Sean Oswald
Donna Z. Meredith
Erica Penttila
Steve Backhus
Yara Cluver
Aaron J Cowan
Kate Tepe
Lori Davis
Mark Mussman
Rush Whitacre
Molly Quanty
James Rotz
Miya Tokumitsu
Sarah Blyth-Stephens
Nick Stange
Michael Bush
Stacey Thomas
Hunter Stamps
Andrew Au
Bryeanne Summers
Lesley A. Martin
Rebecca Najdowski
Jesse Sherbune
Greg Stahly
Derek Parker
Tim Hailey
Noel Anderson
Joel Wright
Jamie Buchsbaum
Randy Young
Jessie Kemp
Christopher Schneberger
Dana Sperry
Michelle Rozic
Rebecca Litt
Jim Broccolo
Saeide Kmi
Fazilat Soukhakian

Jane Alden Stevens
Grant Goodall
Shane Harris
Melanie Frakes
Flavia Bastos
John Neborak
Kelley Ledge
Kelly O'Malley
Matt Distel
Maureen Roberts Miller
Nina Biermann
Georgia Kay Strange
Ian Hagarty
Katie Walters
Nathan Purath
Gaby Cheikh
Brigid O'Kane
Natalie Jenkins
Kim Paice
Alma Alloro
Dan Pribble
Saneeya Ghadially
Helen Toomer
Gsb Gsb
Sara Ludy
Ben Fino-Radin
Jonathan Dankenbring
Martin Kohout
Abby Urban
Caroline Barcella
Russell Tyler
Mark Edward Kelley Dorf
Zach Nader
Shawn C. Smith
Kevin O Mooney
Jeffrey Wolin
Jaime Thompson
Frank Hibrandt
Alexandra Gorczynski
Michelle Murphy
Carlyn Kiniyalocts
A Bill Miller
Jason Huff
Rasmus Emanuel Svensson
Lucy Curzon
Travis Shaffer
Ania Urbanski
Osamu James Nakagawa
Megan Marie Myers
Casey Wilson
Benjamin Schmitt

TransientProjectsToPeople
Lindsay Howard
Johan Rosenmunthe
Brian Harper
Nicolas Sassoon
Merrilee Luke-Ebbeler
Supermassive Blackhole
Jenny Roesel Ustick
Vicki Daiello
Lauren Atkinson
Katie Hyde
Steph Davidson
Emily Rose Cmar
Joseph Yølk Chiocchi
Stacey Griffin Hallahan
Joelle Dietrick
Alfredo Salazar-Caro
Ann Woo
Joshuah Miller
Dennis Kowalski
Maja Dabrowska
Denise Burge
Peter Happel Christian
Scott Sturgill
Kim Asendorf
Charles Negre
Jaakko Pallasvuo
Zoë Salditch
Silvia Lorenz
Sarah Marcella Casnellie
Mac Shafer
Barry Stone
Anastasia Samoylova
Kurtis Denne
Jennifer Chan
Jonathan Gitelson
David Kaplan
Matthew Borths
Galo MoncayoAsan
Libby Rowe
Jason Lazarus
Kate Elliott
Jeremiah Johnson
L. Aili Schmeltz
Captain Gingersnap
Amanda Lee Anderson
Laurel Schwulst
Ross L. Gould
Anne Massoni
David Everett
Julie Stoermer

Lorna Mills
Laurie Kang
Adam Cruces
Kate Wenderfer
Chris Collins
Juliette Bonneviot
Carré Blanc
Angelo Plessas
Rachel Lundak
Arabella Campbell
Jasper Spicero
Tracy Longley-Cook
Sherwin Rivera Tibayan
Brian Ulrich
Nate Larson
Phil Toledano
Anjali Alm-Basu
Valentina Tanni
Jimmy Baker
Stephen Slaughter
Ben Tanzer
Joel Whitaker
Ben Alper
Mike Wsol
Steve Kemple
Shane Parker
Thomas Cheneseau
Jon Feinstein
Krist Wood
Jason Burton Johnson
James Schenck
Omry Middle Keren
Ché Zara Blomfield
Lauri Lynnxe Murphy
Leah Beeferman
John Powers
Lindsay Contini
Rodanny Gee
Lauren Pascarella
Trevor Paglen
Jeff O'Brien
Aaron Walker
Jay Gould
Hugo Scibetta
Chase Bowman
Derek Frech
Ryan Mulligan
Zachary Davis
Natalie Hegert
Nate Smyth
Chelsea Baker

Emily Boswell Wenzler
Marcus Ahlers
Minh-Ha T. Pham
Matthew Gamber
Katia Michel
Nick DeMarco
Emily Colucci
Mike Donahue
Nat Ward
Catherine McCurry
Jess Ramsay
Elisa Zhang
Lisa YingYing Chen
Domenico de Chirico
Jenny Yoo
Corwin Peck
Sara Ludin
Jill Van Epps
Christopher Clubb
Bea Fremderman
Charita 'Flener' Lovitt
Wyatt Niehaus
JE Macián
Guthrie Lonergan
Corrina Mehiel
Conner Ross Green
Seyhan Musaoglu
Leslie Sharpe
Jane Tam
Gordon Holden
Erin Davis
Keith Colclough
Marco Allodi
Timur Si-Qin
Faith Holland
Margaret Dolinsky
Spencer Longo
Sam Falls
Leah Schrager
Laura Brothers
Sean Stewart
Travis Hallenbeck
D.w. Turner
Vincent Chen
Craig Moyer
Ryder Ripps
Juliet Manto
Katie Bakarich
Chris Thompson
Mark Essen
Travess Smalley

Jacob D. Stein
Christopher Schreck
Beth Noe
Philip Spangler
Julia Housiaux
Amelia Morris
Eric Gordon
Emiline Sites
John Transue
Billy Rennekamp
Curtis Mann
Jeffrey Cortland Jones
Halley Espy Kropa
Grant Willing
Ryan Barone
Barry Andersen
Pete Voelker
Krystal South
Kari Altmann
Ben Valentine
Marysa Marderosian
Justin Kemp
Kasey Hosp
Lili Huston-Herterich
Michael Ruiz
Damon Zucconi
Ren Cummings
Joe Lacina
Allyson Anne Lamb
Ryan Tudor
Alex Ross
Daniel Shea
Rob Southard
Mark Beasley
Petra Cortright
James Clarkson
Josefer Sánchez
Sanja Lukač
Zach Searcy
Will Brand
Adam Ferriss
Patricia Murphy
Mark Byron
Drury Peregrine
Rachel Valinsky
Sarah Khatcherian Milo
Tabor Robak
Micah Schippa
Daniel Wallace
Brian Droitcour
Aureliano Segundo

Katy Whitt
Harry Griffin
Derek Dix
Nicolas Stefano Pedde Lay
Andreas Wagner
Nikki S. Lee
Dave Greber
Jon Rafman
Philippe Riss
Britta Thie
Alexis Stahl
Tyler Los-Jones
Daniel Rehn
Tema Stauffer
Michael R.
Simon Denny
Jenna Miller
Amy Stevens
Chris Harvey
Rubén Elyn Reyes
Rick Wolhoy
Matt Barton
McNair Evans
Jennilee Marigomen
Catherine Richards
Casey Rubenok
Viviane Sassen
Craig Courtney
Alison Taylor
Aleph Escobedo
Richard Nikl
Joe Hamilton
Riyo Nemeth
David Rosenthal
Joel Cook
Jessica Mccarrel
Flemming Ove Bech
Érik Spínola
Lauren Cornell
Roy Ascott
Justin Kelly
Myriam Ziehli
Theo Mullen
Mathieu Lcmc
Rhys Coren
Jacob Broms Engblom
Lara Nguyen
Guido Segni
Will Becker
Christina J Massey
Lemya El Sophia

Domenico Dom Barra
Dean Mclean
Asli Serbest
Rebekah Modrak
Alice Charlotte Ray
Michael Jones McKean
Ariel Shanberg
Phil Thompson
Penelope Umbrico
Richard Healy
Mitch Trale
Karen Archey
okey okey
Nik Kosmas
Susan Kae Grant
Todd Frahm
Laura Moses
Nancy Leticia
Noel Rodo-Vankeulen
Johnny Crash
Organ Armani
Balthazar Berling
Katja Mater
Aleksandra Domanović
Loïq Sutte
Barbara Houghton
Caitlin Denny
Scott Klang
Jen McVeigh
Emilio Gomariz
Nikoo Nooryani
Charlotte Gregory
Thomas Hellstrom
Chajana Denharder
Jonah Porter
Joel Holmberg
Lotta Hedberg
Mitch Posada
Daito Manabe
William Sneddon
Brrian Kokoska
Etienne Garachon
Bernard Gauthier
Manu Blondiau
Brooks Dierdorff
Brent Lashley
Kasia Gumpert
Jayson Musson
Andrew Jeffrey Wright
Keko Jackson
Jef Bouillot

Jen Bekman
Sorawit Songsataya
Pierre-Arnaud Doucède
Maryanne Casasanta
Harlan Erskine
Michael Fiday
William Roy Hodgson
Erica Allen
Wm M Harvey
Ceci Moss
Livia Corona
Achim Mohné
Nathan Baker
Rachel Elizabeth Seed
Zacharia Hamideche
Timothée Chaillou
Jonas Lund
Hollis Hammonds
Krista Wortendyke
Mary Scott
Lily Ellender Parmenter
Kuba Ryniewicz
Wojciech Kosma
Michael Tabeling
Ryan Lydon
Pascual Sisto
Ashland Mines
Ed Fornieles
Enrico Boccioletti
Rita McKeough
JoAnna Ford
Kenichi Matsumoto
Corey Hallahan
Jack Joseph Kahn
John Blake Knechtel
Débora Delmar
Gregory Laynor
Elizabeth Sherburne
Crapaud Melle
Georges Jacotey
Pxvl Bxrsch
Cheon Lee
Shunya Hagiwara
Melvin Tan
Nina Wenhart
Jennifer Walke
Rod Barton
Daniel Temkin
Brunco Ceschel
Charalampos Kydonakis
Andy Marko

Timothy Briner
Anne de Vries
Casey Reas
Phillip Maisel
Bill Sullivan
Emilie Gervais
Jan Robert Leegte
Vvork Book
Michael Staniak
Sara Geist
Sally McKay
Joe Meiser
Jerome Saint-Clair
Fabian Golban Tabibian
Masako Sayer
Loraine Wible
Yuri Pattison
Collin Zipp
Jacob Carson
Priti Nilisha Sharma
Jeff Nilan
Amani Olu
Amanda Heil Hodapp
Christopher B Peckham
Luc Hyo Myoung Kim
Lucas Blalock
Nicholas Arnold
Annabelle Arlie
Niko Princen
S.e. Steele
Lauren Payne
Lauren Black
Arjun Ram Srivatsa
Constant Dullaart
Zachary Shay Hüber
Maxime Guyon
Nick Briz
Karlos Gil
Taryn Simon
Martijn Hendriks
Joni Younkins-Herzog
Jessica Mallios
Ellie Pyle
John Calvelli
Corinna Kirsch
Adriana Ramić
Meg Maggio
Roy Avitak
Jan Khür
S.c. Artroom
Taylor Holland

Gabbi Lanza
Thaddeus Kellstadt
Onn Supasiri S
Jennifer Helen Krivickas
Basak Malone
Molta Gente
Guillaume Maraud
Meg Mitchell
Helen Ad
Saoirse Wall
Vicki Sher
David Dillon
Ali Hina
Claudio Marcelo Iglesias
Philippe Spigolon
Brian Khek
Vitor Aiolfi
Darlin Lozano
Margaret Stratton
Jeff Gardocki
Karina Sibata
Eric Fleischauer
Fabrizio Affronti
Yoshi Sodeoka
Joey Versoza
Aaron Sage
André Carlos Lenox-Samour
Joshua Montoya
Giselle Zatonyl
Masood Kamandy
Baptist Penetticobra
Alex Von Bergen
Collin Avery
John Michael Boling
Shane Mecklenburger
Elena Radice
Samuel T. Adams
Art Damage
Christopher Gianunzio
Kim Shifflett
Amelia Daniel Stamps
Jake Urbanski
Sharareh Khosravani
Rebecca R Peel
Errore Zine
Allison Ventura
Amalia Ulman
Bunny Rogers
Otto Prod
Chris Vorhees
J.d. Walsh

John Sousa
Parker Ito
Evan Paschke
Jacob Ciocci
Gabrichidze Nick
Matt Morris
Christian Hendricks
Sheida Soleimani
Crista Dix
Ruthie Myers
Eric Shaw
Andy Holtin
Marcus Isiah Bradshaw
Jackson Xoxo
Savash Erenler
Monica America PearTree
Anastasiya Yatsuk
Marco Strappato
Matthew Landry
Michael Vincent Rainero
Sean Joseph Patrick
Carney
Jenna Wade
Ann Segal
Chase Melendez
Brett Westerman
Makz Ztoz
Andrey Bogush
Leah Stahl
Mario Zoots
Giuseppe Pinto
Jeremy Tubbs
David Andrew Frey
Faith Latorre
Andrea Indini
Sarah Weis
Chris Mullins
Rick Herzog
Sudeep Halappa
Matei Samihaian
Thomas Albdorf
Paul Brown
Lazaro Souza
Enda O'Donoghue
Emily Hanako Momohara
Francesco Cagnin
Dennis DeHart
Rob Off
Bryan Krueger
Brad Tinmouth
Eric Shows

Tatiana Leshkina
Michael Bell-Smith
Will Eagle
Brandon Reddell
Linda Schwartz
Lance Wakeling
Michelle Ceja
Khush Nubian
Alex Risch
Rachel Lynn Zubrowski
Kristin Lucas
Jasper Elings
Siavash Yansori
Stephan Backes
John Cairns
Brandon Juhasz
Andy Powell
Theodore Darst
Joshua Ramirez
Peter Erickson
Eric T. White
Piet Mondriaan
Eltons Kūns
Andrew Rosinski
Sebastian Schmieg
Skyler Schubert
Gregory Hubbard
Emily Jones
T-arte Tatin
Lauren Post
Manny Palou
Zora Tine
Dean Ha
Andreas Schimanski
Maximilian Greyscale
Robert Lorayn
Jean-Philippe Ronnan
Peter Puklus
Dominik Podsiadly
Matt Siber
Tim Berresheim
Item Videogramo
Hendrik Niefeld
Christopher Rauschenberg
Mari Seda-Reeder
Raphaela Platow
Kasem Nakarat
Hekkah Awr
Françoise Gamma
Rhett Jones
Kyle Laidig

Agente Doble
Marilyn Hicks
Nuno Patricio
Alice Et-Mattia
Betty Griffin
Primitibo Ako
Jessica Ankeney
Adam Welch
Inti Romero
Michael A Weber
Pegy Zali
Allisonrob Tanner
Charlie Woodman
Kelli Connell
Raum No
Ciro Museres
Vajza N'kuti
Jaap Drupsteen
IncredibleMoutainOfnewMedia
Miyö Van Stenis
Jahvier Peretz
Melinda Topilko
Latorretta Sulborgo
Arthur Brum
Etudesbooks Etudes
Mike Francis
Brenna Murphy
Manuel Fernández
Émilie Marchand
Esteban Ottaso
Idgi Guy
Richard Skylar
Mika Aabraham
Hideki Fukada
Filippo Lorenzin
Eva Natland
Roy Hutchinson
Jimmy Junk
Neal Sjolin
Inma Femenia
Ronny Szillo
Speed Show
Jasper Elings
Debora Delmar Corp
Khaled Galaleldeen
Ki̇ller Insti̇nct
Vasily Zaitsev
Ashley Peel Pinkham
Jordie Cluny
Raul Altosaar
Emiliano Aversa

Lewk Wilmshurst
Systaime Alias Michaël Borras
Hikari Nakagawa
Pn Ensba
App Tester
David Dao Ellena
Broken Dayton
Peter Le Bek
Mattie Hillock
Kamilia Kard
Evan Drolet Cook
David Lester
Gregg Newman
Pera Lopez
Thomas Hemmings
Viva-Good Wibes
Nico Nicolas
Duodezimalsys Tem
Shingo Tsubouchi
LosAngeles ArtResource
Moises Sanabria
Bianca Monroe
Envoyenterprises Les
Felix Luque
Vog Fontaine
Matmos Press
Tom Sguir
New Dennis Knopf
Fotomagazin Der Greif
Disko Zap
El Corbusier
Birgit Krause
Best Wall Cover
Mulford Tightner
LaTurbo Avedon
Nina Beier
Ikea Glass
Sara Jo Schultz
Mathilde Soan
Dot Dot
Chris Brown
Benjamin Schmuck
Kit Kittens
Bill Hussy
Yuki Tomita
Anton KernGallery
Km Temporaer
Monica Williams
Amiti Brookes
Léa Poinsignon

Mary Iles
A Black Jpeg
Morry Mathaway
Pro Art Research-Crew
Theo Contemprelics Ries
Mauzy Virginia
Jon Yamashiro
Avg Exorcist
Luc Fuller
Ton Awe
Océane Picard
Aggtelek Duo
Britney Rivers
Jack le Lo
Kutay Cengil
Trudie Smith
Ingo Mittelstaedt
Ivana Pashmore
Naomi Curd
David Rickard's
Jonathan Chacón
Perennial Melt
Jeremy Bailey-TheArchive
Jul Candy
Retrospective Hudson
Anthony Crch
Betty Griffin
Alex Woodman
Discovering Borderlands
Gregory Kalliche
Judah Silverstone
Michael Smith
Pratibh Trivedi Praative
Chris Coy
Popup Cincy
Justin Hodges
Thavma Collectiva
George Hoffman
Orina Juazy
Rat Polle
Lisa Fox
Ashlan Musante
Interstate BK

This publication was conceived to accompany the group exhibition *Ambients*, curated by Rachel Valinsky, featuring Sean Thomas Blott, Andrew Durbin, Eileen Maxson, Aiden Morse, Wyatt Niehaus, Corwin Peck, and Jordan Tate, on view from February 13 through March 16, 2014 at Peninsula Art Space in Red Hook, Brooklyn. *Friends* is available in an unlimited print on demand edition. The text is set in Casper, a free font designed by Michael Chereda. Cover design and typesetting by Claire Sammons.

www.ingramcontent.com/pod-product-compliance
Lightning Source LLC
Chambersburg PA
CBHW051817170526
45167CB00005B/2049